Shaggy Chic

Shaggy Chic

Fetching Makeovers for Any Dog

JANET PRUSA AND COCO

Avon, Massachusetts

Published by Adams Media, an F + W Publications Company
57 Littlefield Street
Avon, MA 02322
www.adamsmedia.com

 A QUIRK PACKAGING BOOK

Photography by Frank Heckers, except the following pages photos courtesy
of the dogs' owners: 10, 14, 18, 26, 42, 46, 50, 54, 58, 62, 66, 70, 74, 78, 82, 86
Art Direction by Lynne Yeamans
Edited by Signe Bergstrom and Sarah Scheffel
Designed by Stephanie Stislow

ISBN 10: 1-59869-434-0
ISBN 13: 978-1-59869-434-5

Printed in China

J I H G F E D C B A

This book is available at quantity discounts for bulk purchases.
For information, please call 1-800-289-0963.

To Ryan, Katie, and Weenie Wobbles

I would sincerely like to thank my friends at Quirk Packaging for understanding my sense of whimsy and letting me get carried away with it. Thank you, Frank, for never questioning a dog's outfit. I am especially grateful to all my dog talent and to their wonderful owners who trusted me and took the time to get involved in the *Shaggy Chic* adventure. I would like to express many thanks to Beth Groubert from American Rat Terrier Rescue and to local pet detective Jane Colton and Tina Mulvey, for scouting the greatest dogs for me. Finally, I am so appreciative of Jeff Silverstein and Frank Foronjy, owners of Raising Rover for providing *Shaggy Chic* with the most glamorous outfits money can buy.

Contents

Introduction

My experience as a stylist to dogs goes back to the early days of my childhood. As a budding fashionista, I wasn't content to merely style my friends' wardrobes or cut their hair. My makeovers extended all the way to our family poodle, Lulu. Poor Lulu—I subjected her to the most humiliating getups, outfitting her in my little sister's swimming cap, my cowgirl boots, and layers upon layers of necklaces "liberated" from my mother's jewelry case. Lulu, for her part, was a very patient pup and accepted my attentions with great aplomb. Too bad I can't say the same for my sis or mom. Several years later, I graduated to the big city, New York, and focused my designing eye on more willing human models. Then I met Coco.

While styling the wardrobe for a fashion shoot, I noticed something moving behind the racks of clothing. Upon closer inspection, I saw a fuzzy white puppy who had somehow gotten herself tangled up in a Chanel scarf. When she triumphantly emerged, the scarf was draped smartly across her small head. She was picture perfect, and I wondered if her fashion sense was so innate, so instinctual, that she had actually planned the whole scenario.

"Who is this?" I asked, cradling the pup in my hands. "Does she belong to anyone?" Before anyone could reply, I already knew the answer to my own question: She belonged to me. Of course, I had to name her Coco.

Since that fateful day, Coco and I have been inseparable. Beyond companionship, we also share a unique flair for fashion and an uncanny ability to make over the least likely candidates: dogs. Coco and I have transformed the mangy to the marvelous on more than one occasion. Now, we are proud to have the opportunity to reveal our methods. *Shaggy Chic: Fetching Makeovers for Any Dog* unveils the step-by-step processes we employ to make any dog runway ready.

The best makeovers are more than just hair-deep. We are frequently called in, either by friends or family members, to help a pooch and his or her human companion deal with a behavioral issue that manifests itself in a physical light. Take Otto, for example. An overweight English bulldog, Otto beseeched us to transform him from spud to stud. It took more than designer duds to change this pup from a Slothario to a Romeo; with a comprehensive diet and exercise plan, Otto's makeover was a true lifestyle change. Sometimes, a makeover seems all about glitter and glam, as with Lana, a pug who had to face the red carpet for an awards ceremony. This makeover was really about building confidence, however. Coco and I went for a dazzling look, and Lana truly felt like an award winner.

Have we ever faced a canine who was resistant to change? Yes, and we responded with lots of positive reinforcement and treats!

The secret to a great makeover is to assess each situation based on the unique personalities, needs, desires, and capabilities of the dog and her human. Whether your pooch needs her look refreshed just a bit or is ready for a dramatic change, the process of making the change will benefit you both. Every mutt (canine or human) deserves a chance to accentuate her best qualities, unleash her inner doggie diva, and know what it is to look her best.

Shaggy Chic is divided into twenty chapters, featuring one makeover per chapter. For each pup, a before photo and profile reveal the particular challenges posed by the makeover. Then we discuss the steps Coco and I took to make the changes, and reveal the dramatic results! Throughout, you'll find helpful grooming tips and practical words of wisdom to spiff up any pup. We've also included a thorough Resources section to help you find our favorite products, stores, and services.

It is our hope that these makeover stories will inspire you and your pooch: Here's to the dog's life!

XOX,

Janet and Coco
New York City

before
prematurely old

**ALTHOUGH MAXINE'S ENERGY
IS STILL HIGH, HER OLD LOOK
NEEDS TO BE RETIRED.**

pooch profile

meet Maxine, a golden retriever from Virginia who acts as nanny to the children of the house.

likes Playing with pups and children, and listening to her owner's voice as she reads children's bedtime stories.

dislikes The wind and being left alone.

the challenge To add a youthful glow to Maxine's golden years, we need to add style and subtract dog years.

the solution A makeover that makes Maxine look youthful, without disguising her well-earned signs of age.

lesson learned New tricks add verve to an older dog's life.

Turn Back the Clock

PRUDENT MAXINE RECLAIMS HER YOUTH

With age comes great wisdom. But does wisdom have to be accompanied by gray hair? Even though Maxine feels feisty and vivacious, her appearance is beginning to look more "olden" than golden. For this pooch, a youthful appearance is easy to retrieve—with a little help from some experts, of course.

the back story

Maxine has a ways to go before she hits the AARF age but she looks older than her actual age of ten. Other owners frequently mistake her for a seriously senior dog, never mind that she can still run with the best of them. Her once golden mane of hair has started to turn white prematurely, and her demeanor is that of an older dog.

With a house full of youngsters, Maxine's owners needed a dog that would be good with children; her stable personality seemed like a perfect fit. And so it turned out—Maxine is the model of patience, a real-life Nana, straight out of *Peter Pan*. Years later, however, Maxine needs a magical makeover to restore the luster of youth. I have a feeling that this pooch won't object to a day of pampering. After all, every dog deserves her day. "There's no time like the present to get this makeover running like clockwork," I say, and prepare our makeover plan.

Our goal is to rejuvenate Maxine's look. Her owners, however, have a tricky request: They want us to leave her dignified white temples untouched. Even Coco gets her grays touched-up every now and again. And I wouldn't look half my age without my monthly visits to Curl Up and Dye, my favorite hair salon. But for Maxine, Coco and I are willing to try some alternative solutions to turn back the hands of time.

I remember the old adage, "You are only as old as you feel." Even though I don't know how Maxine feels, her eyes shine with a youthful glimmer. Hmmm, I wonder if Maxine really is a model of youth. With that in mind, I grab my day planner and get to work: Maxine will be a picture-perfect reflection of youthful vigor and enthusiasm in no time!

after aging gracefully

MAXINE, IN A FETCHING, YOUTHFUL ENSEMBLE.

the makeover

Time waits for no pup. In order to beat the clock, Coco and I have to unlock the secrets of youth . . . and fast.

1. First stop: the grooming salon. Since we can't touch the white in Maxine's hair, we decide to update her hair-style with a trim. With the weight of all that excess hair lifted, Maxine will instantly feel more sprightly. The groomer uses straight scissors to snip the hair around Maxine's face, and shapes her mane to frame her bright eyes. This cut draws attention away from her white streaks. As a gentle reminder of youthful days, the groomer chooses baby-scented powder shampoo to wash Maxine's thick coat.

2. To confirm Maxine's inner youthfulness, we visit the veterinarian, who gives Maxine a thorough exam. After receiving a clean bill of health, the doc prescribes a program of regular exercise—the best way to stay young is to stay active. Both of Maxine's owners take a weekly yoga class, so I scheduled a doga class (see Resources: Exercise)—partner yoga between owner and dog—so everyone can practice Chaturanga and Downward-Facing Dog poses together.

3. To give her coat a healthy glow, Coco and I suggest daily snacks of carrot sticks and supplemental vitamin powder—Missing Link Omega 3 is a great brand (see Resources: Food and Vitamin Supplements).

4. The kids love to dress Maxine up in doll clothes and cast-off school uniforms, but we decide her wardrobe should reflect her station in life. We select timeless accessories, including stylish tortoiseshell sunglasses and a colorful but tastefully printed scarf.

5. Pampering brings out the pup in all of us, so we treat Maxine to a day at a doggie spa. Knowing that she is probably sore from doga, we give her an hour-long massage session. We know she's relaxed when the therapist confides that she has fallen asleep on the table.

When we return Maxine to her home, she enthusiastically greets the children, and before we can count to three, they have outfitted her in her new wardrobe. Just as they finish, Maxine lets out a joyous howl and does three Chaturangas in a row. Her hair is still white but her personality is all pup.

COCO'S TIPS ARF!

CARING FOR AN OLDER DOG

• *Massage your senior dog daily (see Resources: Exercise). Start at the top of the head and slowly stroke down the back to the base of the tail three to four times.*

• *Supplements, like glucosamine, will ease arthritic pain. Senior pooches should get twice-yearly checkups since they are particularly susceptible to disease.*

before eternal optimist

**OLIVER SEARCHING
FOR A WHIFF OF LOVE.**

pooch profile

meet Oliver, a four-year-old French bulldog who attracts love wherever he goes.

likes Stealing tennis balls, sleeping in the crook of anyone's knees, pet stores that give out free treats, and golden retrievers.

dislikes Cars.

the challenge Can Oliver sniff out Mr. Right for his owner?

the solution Get out and get noticed!

lesson learned Look for love in the right places (a dog run is a good bet for dog and owner alike)!

Laws of Attraction

A FRENCHIE MAKES A MATCH

It's tough to meet people in the big city. Oliver's owner should know.
She's lost hope that she'll ever find Mr. Right. Trusting Oliver's instincts more
than her own, she's decided to let Oliver select her next beau. After all,
he is a French bulldog. Hopefully, he can sniff out l'amour.

the back story

Oliver knows about love firsthand. Raised on a farm in Virginia before moving to New York City, he grew up frolicking in the countryside with several litters of Frenchies. He was the breeder's favorite and spent every night indoors curled up in her bed. She bought him special toys and showered him with affection. Oliver grew up to be an affectionate, caring dog.

When he's not chasing leggy golden retrievers, Oliver is the consummate matchmaker for everyone else. Perhaps his warm upbringing guaranteed his luck in love. Or perhaps it was his French stock. Whatever the reason, his special skill is undeniable. While Oliver's owner hasn't been so fortunate in the dating world, several of her friends have scored with her pup's help: Amy and Brian met when they stopped to admire Oliver. Mary and Tom were married a year after Oliver enticed them to play ball in the park. Can Oliver make it a triple?

Even though Oliver's owner has just about given up, and even Oliver is beginning to doubt his matchmaking abilities, we know that timing is everything and opportunity is everywhere. Our makeover will include ideas on how to vary their routine—let's stir things up a little!—and ensure that their routine crosses paths with plenty of available men.

And, of course, since there are throngs of becoming pup-and-female sets on the city streets vying for male attention, Oliver and his owner need to be dressed to attract attention. Oliver's owner is as chic as can be; she needs no help from us in that department. And, although we have to admit that Oliver is already naturally stylish, we plan to throw a little *je ne sais quoi* into the mix to accentuate his attraction factor.

after modern-day cupid

EVERYDAY IS VALENTINE'S DAY FOR OLIVER.

the makeover

Let the matchmaking games begin!

1. Oliver needs to look dashing for their daily walks. Luckily, French bulldogs are easy to maintain, unlike their English cousins. A quick brush removes the dead hair and skin and leaves his coat shiny and odorless. We also examine Oliver's ears to make sure they are nice and pink and quickly swipe them with a cotton swab.

2. Most Frenchies dislike having their nails clipped. In fact, they don't even like having their paws touched. Luckily, Oliver's breeder touched his ears and paws while praising him when he was a pup. Today, he doesn't object one bit during our nail-clipping session.

3. To ensure Oliver's breath smells as good as he looks, we give his teeth and tongue a thorough brushing using Petrodex Enzymatic Toothpaste (see Resources: Beauty). We even surprise him with a tin of all-natural Yip Yap breath freshener—just the thing for any pooch looking to smooch.

4. Finally, we replace Oliver's practical navy blue leash with a heart-patterned one. With this final flourish in place, Oliver and his owner are ready for their man hunt. We make a reservation at a nearby French café, where they can dine outside. To work off the meal, we suggest a sunset stroll through the park. Although no dashing suitor is discovered, by the end of the evening, Oliver's owner feels optimistic about her prospects.

And well she should: Thanks to Oliver and a little help from two covert stylists, Oliver's owner soon meets the man of her dreams at the neighborhood dog run. And the best part? He owns a golden retriever, so Oliver finds a little love, too. Love has come full circle for Oliver!

COCO'S TIPS
THE HEART-HEALTHY POOCH

HERE'S HOW TO KEEP HIS TICKER IN TIP-TOP SHAPE.

- *Never let your dog nibble chocolate. It contains a stimulant called theobromine that is poisonous to dogs. Instead, try all-natural carob treats, like those from Bubba Rose Biscuit Company (see Resources: Food and Vitamin Supplements).*

- *Select heart-healthy treats for your dog. Fresh fruits, vegetables, and multi-grains are good choices.*

- *While treatment of canine heartworm disease is usually successful, prevention of the disease is much safer and more economical. Chose from monthly tablets, chewables, and topicals.*

courting romance

**AFTER THEIR FIRST PLAY DATE, THEY
KNEW IT WAS A PERFECT MATCH.**

pooch profile

meet Bella and Jasper, a pair of two-year-old purebred Chihuahuas who found puppy love through the slots of a picket fence.

likes Bella enjoys lounging in the sun, while Jasper is a water enthusiast.

dislikes The lawn mower and weed whacker are lethal enemies number one and two.

the challenge First comes love . . . then comes marriage. Since these pups already have love (not to mention a house with a picket fence), it's time to plan a fabulous wedding.

the solution Formal attire and a magnificent cake set the stage.

lesson learned Love really can conquer all!

A Dream Wedding

PUPTIALS PENDING

These pampered Chihuahuas have every luxury they could possibly want—from designer beds to gourmet treats. Unfortunately, they're missing key ingredients to a life of happiness: each other. Separated by a fence that divides their backyards, they yearn to find a way to be together.

the back story

Bella and Jasper's biggest predicament: how to cross that pesky fence so they can enjoy one-on-one playtime? No matter what they do to communicate their wish to their owners—Bella tries howling, while Jasper jumps up and down—their pleas are misunderstood. Their owners simply shush them, or think they are objecting to the weather and bring them indoors. If they took a moment's pause, however, they would realize that their pups are running themselves ragged in an effort to break through that picket fence.

Finally, one serendipitous morning, Bella's usual stroll is rerouted and the Chihuahuas—and their owners—meet face-to-face. Bella and Jasper sniff each other with abandon and romp as much as their leashes allow. We hear that they even touch noses—Bella and Jasper, that is. Their owners exchange pleasantries and decide that the pups should have a play date that coming weekend.

From that weekend on, Bella and Jasper play together every Saturday and Sunday. For a couple of fun-packed hours, they are allowed to run and tumble together, barrier free. But when it's time to go home, they are as distressed as can be. The contrast does not escape their owners' notice: clearly, their pups have fallen in love, and it's time to take action. They tear down the white picket fence and replace it with some low-maintenance ivy. Now, Bella and Jasper can enjoy each other's company whenever they want. To celebrate the happy union, their owners decide to plan an even happier one: a wedding for Bella and Jasper.

As you may have guessed, the ceremony will take place in the ivy patch where the fence used to be. But the owners quickly realize that a wedding, even for two small pooches, involves a lot of details. They turn to Coco and me to plan the joyous occasion.

after a lifetime of happiness

BELLA AND JASPER DECORATE THEIR OWN WEDDING CAKE.

the makeover ❀

Throwing a stylish wedding for pups is not all that different from planning a wedding for a human bride and groom.

1. First thing's first: we make a to-do list and delegate, delegate, delegate. Jasper's owner mows the lawn and Bella's trims the ivy. They also draft a short list of guests for us to invite.

2. Two weeks before the big day, we order a traditional wedding cake and a case of bubbly for the owners' friends. Tasty, hand-decorated cookies will be provided for the four-legged guests (see Resources: Food and Vitamin Supplements).

3. Choosing Bella and Jasper's wedding attire is the next priority. Many pet boutiques stock wedding gowns and tuxedos for all sizes of dogs, but we chose to order these sweet little numbers online (see Resources: Fashion and Accessories).

4. Of course, Bella and Jasper must look their best for this special occasion. Lucky for us, their owners give them baths every six to eight weeks and brush them regularly with a grooming glove. They need only a wipe down with a damp cloth to get them ready for the event.

5. Finally, the big day arrives! Eight friends and four small dogs arrive at two o'clock. Bella and Jasper's owners perform a light-hearted ceremony and then their guests indulge in the dog treats, mouth-watering wedding cake, and, of course, champagne.

All involved agreed that the wedding was a perfect celebration of the puppy love that inspired it. Our best wishes to the petite bride and groom!

COCO'S TIPS ARF!
A HARMONIOUS HOUSEHOLD

WHAT HAPPENS WHEN THE TABLES ARE TURNED AND DOGS ARE BROUGHT TOGETHER THROUGH THEIR OWNERS' MARRIAGE? HERE ARE SOME TIPS TO CREATING A LASTING PEACE.

- *When introducing two dogs, choose a neutral location. Keep them both on leashes and let them sniff each other for starters, or you may want to keep the newcomer in a crate until the other dog gets used to him.*

- *If the introductions don't go smoothly, contact a professional animal behaviorist. Dog fights can cause serious injuries.*

- *Always make sure the dogs remember who the pack leader is: you. Let them know that you and your new spouse will not tolerate aggressive behavior.*

before *eager to please*

HARLEY AS THE TEACHER'S PET.

pooch profile

meet Harley, a two-year-old Maltese mix born in Upstate New York. Although undeniably a mama's boy, Harley has a penchant for creating the occasional good-natured ruckus.

likes Paperbacks and nibbling the red pie pieces of Trivial Pursuit.

dislikes The smell of erasers.

the challenge Harley's lack of style may be fine when he's hiding behind a book, but it's time for him to get schooled in the art of fashion.

the solution We'll bring out the bad boy in this unassuming doggie.

lesson learned You can rewrite the ending of any tale!

A Novel Makeover

BOOKWORM GETS UPGRADED TO COOL KID

With a name like Harley, you'd think that this pup hangs out with a gang of bikers. Instead, he prefers spending time with his owner at the library. Harley plays the part of bookworm, but Coco and I suspect he's a wild child underneath. Our goal? Help Harley start a new chapter in life.

the back story

Every weekday morning, Harley hops inside the basket attached to his owner's Schwinn bicycle and accompanies him to the college library. Unless you're one of the three students that visit the library, you've probably never met Harley. He's usually snuggled into a ball behind a stack of new releases or stretched out for a nap beneath the water fountain. Whenever his owner returns books to the shelves, Harley dutifully follows, just to be sure that every title is returned to its appropriate section.

Harley may have everyone else fooled with his A-plus behavior, but Coco and I surmise that he's born to be wild! Beneath his floppy hair and bookish demeanor is a cool kid waiting to be unleashed. We decide to ambush Harley one Friday afternoon and find him dozing by the action/adventure books with shreds of paper suspiciously scattered around his tiny body. "Oh, my," we exclaim and

Harley wakes with a start. When he stands, tail between his legs, ripped pieces of a book jacket fall to the ground. The title? *Into the Wild,* torn to bits.

I explain to Harley's owner, a Ph.D. candidate in philosophy, that his pooch is in need of a cool kid makeover. When I hand him our business card, I can't help but notice the tattoo circling his wrist. Hmmm . . . is Harley's owner hiding his wild side, too?

At the studio, we start by clipping the hair covering Harley's big brown eyes. When the pup sees his reflection, Coco and I swear we detect a mischievous glint in his eye. Harley lets out a low growl—his way, I think, of saying thank you. This is merely step one in the path to his full transformation. Soon, we promise, he will be top-dog material.

after *who's the bad boy?*

LOOK OUT TIMBERLAKE, THERE'S A NEW DOG ON THE BLOCK!

the makeover

We are confident that Harley will see himself in a whole new light once our makeover is complete.

1. To encourage Harley to come out of his shell, we send him to a sports club specifically designed for dogs. Besides offering agility and obedience classes (for companions and competition), this club also teaches something known as flyball, a relay race with four dogs on a team (see Resources: Exercise). By the end of the day, Harley is leading his team!

2. Since we already gave Harley a quick trim, we take him to a hip puppy salon for a hand brushing. The groomer applies a light spray of mink oil to loosen Harley's knots. The gentle brushing leaves his fine coat smooth and silky. For a standout finish, the groomer uses a fine-tooth comb to give Harley a few boy band-worthy spikes.

3. Since Harley is sometimes at a loss when it comes time to communicate his needs, we schedule a date with a behaviorist (see Resources: Training) for Harley and his owner. A few sessions with an expert change this dog whisperer into a vocally confident pooch.

4. We are shocked to learn that Harley doesn't own one piece of outerwear. In homage to his namesake motorcycle, we outfit him with a jean vest from Ruff Rider Dog Apparel (see Resources: Fashion and Accessories), a fashion statement that screams, "Live to ride, ride to live."

5. Since we know Harley has developed an unfortunate taste for books, we surprise him with an arsenal of Ruffian brand chew toys (see Resources: Training). These bouncy toys feature distinctive squeaks that should distract him from munching on paperbacks.

Last we saw them, Harley and his owner were looking too cool for school. The doggy basket and Schwinn had been replaced by a Road Hound pet carrier (see Resources: Fashion and Accessories) and a real Harley motorcycle. Looks like Harley's owner upgraded to a life in the fast lane, too.

COCO'S TIPS
GROOMING COARSE-HAIRED DOGS

COCO, A COARSE-HAIRED DOG HERSELF, SHARES HER TRIED-AND-TRUE ADVICE.

- *Regular grooming is required to keep away matting and tangles. A "puppy cut" looks great and is easy to maintain. Simply trim to a one- to two-inch (three- to five- cm) buzz all over.*

- *White dogs often have tear staining around the eyes and snout. So, trim around the ears and beard regularly and keep the face dry and clean.*

before major-league potential

JOEY ENJOYS RUNS IN THE PARK WITH HIS SPORTS-FIXATED OWNER.

pooch profile

meet Joey, an eight-year old American Stafford-shire terrier, born in the Bronx, New York. Now lives on Chicago's not-so-mean streets.

likes Riding in the car, sitting on the stoop with the neighborhood guys, playing in the dog park, and a good cut of steak.

dislikes Baths and losing a game of tug-of-war.

the challenge Convince the guys that we know a couple of pointers that will improve their game.

the solution Trade up the matching jerseys for a more polished but still sporty look.

lesson learned The secret to being a winner is looking like one, too.

Eternal Jock

JOEY REFINES HIS SPORTS-KING IMAGE

Joey is a talented athlete. His owner, a sports enthusiast, thinks it's hilarious to dress Joey in a gold jersey that matches his own. But Coco and I believe that a little fanfare goes a long way. In order to coach these boys into the winner's circle, we've got to convince them that high style matters just as much as high stats.

the back story

While Joey is a natural at every game he's introduced to, his wardrobe has become a major bone of contention both on and off the field. Even though Joey's owner thinks their matching jerseys set the gold standard in style, nothing could be farther from the truth. "They both wear the same old jersey every day," complains his girlfriend. C'mon boys, it's time to retire those numbers!

When we get to the dog park, it isn't difficult to spot Joey and his owner. True to form, they are both sporting gold jerseys. Even from a distance, Coco and I can make out dirt and grass stains on Joey's frayed shirt—and on his owner's, too. We had been warned that even the suggestion of removing their beloved shirts might elicit aggression, so Coco and I come up with a game plan of our own. Luring both boys with the promise of grilled steak, chips, and beer, we quickly have them cornered. Little do they know, another curveball is coming their way . . .

At the studio, the pair is met by a style intervention team. Of course, we have food and drinks waiting (we're not that cruel), but we've also invited friends, family members, and some doggie pals from the local park to participate in our makeover efforts.

Although we ask Joey and his owner to sit down and remain calm, the excitement is too much for Joey. When Coco dares to sniff the edge of his jersey, he begins running in circles, challenging the other dogs to a game. Once Joey has settled down, one by one friends and family confess their distaste for the matching jerseys. Eventually, Joey and his owner accept their friends' criticism and admit defeat. When they finally relinquish their jerseys to us, we know they are ready to step up to the plate.

after a hole in one

JOEY PROVES THAT THERE MAY BE A LITTLE TIGER IN THIS TERRIER.

the makeover

Once separated from their jerseys, these bad boys turn out to be good sports about their makeover.

1. Because Joey and his owner are a close-knit team, we want them to learn to function as each other's eyes and ears. Though both have perfect eyesight, we employ a seeing-eye dog trainer (see Resources: Training) to teach Joey to distinguish the differences between similar looking objects, like a wedge golf club and a putter. Don't worry—it's all part of our makeover plan.

2. Joey has some aggression issues when it comes to toys, so we enroll the pair in behavior boot camp (see Resources: Training). Joey's owner learns that his behavior has been contributing to Joey's displays of aggression. Whenever they played together, he would let Joey win—at everything. Behavior boot camp teaches them both how to enjoy a more level playing field.

3. When we take Joey to our favorite groomer, he notices that Joey has developed a slight rash around his tummy, where the dirty jersey had been rubbing. The groomer uses an oatmeal and tea tree oil-infused shampoo to soothe Joey's skin (see Resources: Beauty).

4. Just to be sure Joey is picture perfect, we take him for a visit to the dentist. She uses a finger brush and ProDental Gel, formulated with natural baking soda and aloe vera to relieve gum irritation (see Resources: Beauty).

5. While Joey is getting primped, Coco and I pick up a set of golf clubs for his owner. We also buy a selection of polo shirts in a rainbow of colors for Joey. Just as we're leaving, we spy the finishing touch: Casual Canine Hooded Sweatshirts (see Resources: Fashion and Accessories). They are too cool to pass up, so we choose an assortment.

Now it's time to put our makeover to the test: we drive the boys to the nearest closed golf course, where their preppy but sporty look fits right in. When Joey's owner asks him if he can bring him a putter, he barks enthusiastically and retrieves the appropriate club. We hope they enjoy their first round of golf together—and many more to come.

COCO'S TIPS ARF!
GUIDELINES TO A GOOD GAME

KEEP THESE TIPS IN MIND WHEN PLAYING WITH AN ATHLETIC POOCH.

• *Rather than focusing on just one strenuous sport, alternate with a less taxing activity, like swimming or walking.*

• *Do not over-stimulate your dog and avoid competing for a prize.*

• *Remember: you decide when the game begins and when it ends.*

pooch profile

meet Pebbles, an eleven-year-old Jack Russell terrier, originally from Brooklyn.

likes Riding shotgun, the smell of laundry detergent, and her next-door neighbor, Sam.

dislikes There's nothing more distressing to Pebbles than fireworks, thunder, and lightning.

the challenge Curbing their spending sprees will be tough. We've got to substitute their shoppers' highs with something more healthy.

the solution Once Pebbles and her owner figure out that there's more to life than a sale, they'll realize that life doesn't have to be so taxing.

lesson learned Forget "shop 'til you drop"— Pebbles and her owner's new motto is "run 'cause it's fun."

The Shopaholic

HEY, BIG SPENDER

Pebbles's owner loves to shop . . . for anything. No store is off limits, especially when it comes to showering Pebbles with presents. While Pebbles adores her owner, she's tired of accompanying her from store to store. She'd rather spend the day in the park. Can we help these two shopaholics before they reach their limits?

the back story

When Pebbles's owner discovered the world of credit cards, she became addicted to shopping. They used to go for morning jogs and romps in the park. As soon as Pebbles's owner got a wallet full of cards, they were more apt to be at Bloomingdale's than at the dog run. Sure, Pebbles is dressed in the finest haute couture in dog styles, but even Coco and I know that there's more to life than designer duds.

Over time, Pebbles's owner has come to view shopping as retail therapy. Whenever she has a bad day (even if it is a bad hair day), she heads to the store, Pebbles in tow. Pebbles has gotten so comfortable with the Bloomingdale's employees that they keep a bowl of treats just for her. They also reserve a dressing room for Pebbles and her owner and, yes, Pebbles often snoozes in there while her owner scours the racks for the prettiest dress. Shopping spree after shopping spree . . . the costs have begun to pile up.

We know what you're thinking: far be it for Coco and I to offer advice on how to curb these shopaholics' habits. In fact, we're in a prime position to share some words with these two since Coco and I are reformed shopaholics ourselves. Even though Pebbles's cashmere lined coat is luxurious, there's no reason to have twelve of them. At heart, dogs' needs are pretty simple. The most that they require is love and a happy home. Once these basics are taken care of, there's no need to substitute contentment with a new purse or a shopping cart full of doggie toys.

We will have to apply a little tough love to teach these shopping buddies how to curb their spending habits. We are confident that we can get them to recognize life's real treasures: each other!

after *frugal fashionista*

PEBBLES HAS LEARNED HOW TO DRESS FOR LESS.

the makeover

It's not bad for Pebbles and her owner to shop every once in a while so long as they have other hobbies, too.

1. We take a trip to Bloomingdale's with Pebbles and her owner to watch these two in action. Once we see how they operate, we can formulate a makeover strategy that won't leave them feeling deprived. As Pebbles's owner checks out the store's most expensive items first, we notice that Pebbles seems bored with their routine. The only time she perks up is when the Bloomingdale's staff greets her. We politely explain to Pebbles's owner that she needs to pay more attention to the pooch and less to the latest designs. Once she realizes how attention starved the dog really is, she vows to indulge Pebbles's affections more than her shopping habits.

2. Even though Pebbles's owner showers her with clothing, collars, and toys, she rarely takes Pebbles to the groomer's salon. We schedule a private session for owner and pooch to receive manis and pedis. Pebbles has her nails painted with Pawlish in a daring red color (see Resources: Beauty).

3. Pebbles's owner rarely lets Pebbles walk around Bloomingdale's. We send the pair to our fitness expert for a consultation. Together, they create a weekly jogging regimen that will help these two literally get back on track. I introduce Pebbles's owner to the wonderful world of online shopping, which cuts down on their shopping time, leaving more time in the day for exercise.

4. Pebbles's owner never buys anything on sale. No wonder her credit card bills are so high! Once we show her how and where to find the best deals, she is ecstatic.

5. While Pebbles and her owner are out for a run, we shop the sales rack for an adorable dress for Pebbles just to prove that quality can be on discount, too. When we present our finds, they are both pleased with the duds.

The last time we saw this pair they were out for a run. They still frequent Bloomingdale's for pleasure, but have discovered that spending a little less on clothing hasn't left them without style.

COCO'S TIPS ARF!
THE NOSE KNOWS

NOSES AREN'T JUST FOR SNIFFING OUT BARGAINS.

A dog's nose is usually cool and moist. A cool, wet nose doesn't necessarily mean the dog is healthy, and a dry, warm nose doesn't necessarily mean she's sick. Taking her temperature is a better way to check for illness.

before
twin city champs

**THEY'RE INSEPARABLE, BUT
ARE THEY INCORRIGIBLE, TOO?**

pooch profile

meet Inseparable twins Minnie and Roy. Although they hail from the heartland, their ancestry can be traced back to Wales.

likes Children, strolling through the biggest mall in North America, sleeping, and eating.

dislikes Heights.

the challenge Minnie and Roy may be royalty in Minnesota, but they're going to need some etiquette lessons and tasteful garb to win the Queen's heart and the Duke's respect.

the solution The twins get a royal makeover before they even RSVP.

lesson learned Even unruly pups can behave when it's time for tea with the queen!

High Tea for Two

A ROYAL INVITATION

"Her Majesty the Queen and his Royal Highness, the Duke of Edinburgh, request the pleasure of Minnie and Roy for tea with their Royal corgis on June 22. Since you will be expected to romp and play, plan on getting a little dirty. Additionally, no curtseys will be necessary. Please RSVP by June 15."

the back story

Appropriately enough, corgi twins Minnie and Roy live in the Twin Cities with their owner. For many years, their owner has longed to "cross the pond" to learn more about her family's Welsh heritage. She's certain Minnie and Roy wouldn't mind the trip. In fact, she suspects that the corgis are every bit as Welsh as she is.

One morning, inspiration strikes: she'll trace Minnie and Roy's family tree. "What if your ancestors belonged to my ancestors?" she wonders aloud. Or what if Minnie and Roy are part of a royal lineage? It is common knowledge that the royal family bred corgis.

Before she can question her impulse, Minnie and Roy's owner dashes off a letter to the queen and encloses a photo of the twins. She begins, "I am writing under the opinion that my corgis look very much like your small brood . . ." And then, she crosses her fingers.

A few weeks later, she receives a reply from the queen that shakes her from her Lazy Boy recliner. "It is with great pleasure that I announce that your twins are related to my corgis." She continues, "I cannot wait to meet our third cousins from across the pond." As their owner twirls around, Minnie and Roy follow suit, running in tight circles.

After the first wave of delight passes, Minnie and Roy's owner pays us a visit in a panic. She knows that her corgis must be respectable and obedient when they meet the queen, but she admits she has never been good at saying "no" to the pair. I eye Minnie, who is rummaging through the wastebasket, while Roy tugs on the corner of a throw blanket. These twins are in no way prepared for crowning glory. It is definitely time for the changing of the guard.

after tea totalers

MINNIE AND ROY LOOKING FIT FOR A KING.

the makeover

Once Minnie and Roy's ruffian behavior is smoothed out, we'll dress them to look the part.

1. Since the pair is in need of some serious discipline, Coco and I turn to an etiquette coach, who tutors the twins on how to behave in a formal social situation (see Resources: Training). Minnie and Roy learn the command for "gentle" so that whenever they accept something new—say a tea biscuit or a scone—they will politely grasp the object in their mouths, rather than quickly snatching it, per their usual style.

2. A trip to the neighborhood groomer ensures that Minnie and Roy's downy, water-resistant overcoats get the royal treatment. Using a wire pin brush, the groomer smooths their straight surface hair, and applies Fur Butter to soften their wavy overcoats (see Resources: Beauty). He then cleans their ears and teeth and trims any excess hair from between their footpads. For a finishing touch, he applies dog-friendly perfume to Minnie and cologne to Roy (see Resources: Beauty). This misting spray helps control pet odor between shampoos and gives off a long-lasting fresh, clean scent.

3. Realizing that their country cousins will most likely be fit as fiddles, we put Minnie and Roy through some rock-jumping training to make sure they can keep up with their kin. By the week's end, Minnie and Roy can do entire laps of the mall and bound through a series of obstacle courses designed to replicate the Welsh terrain.

4. Shopping for the proper attire requires some resourcefulness. The mall doesn't have what we envision, so Coco and I commission a seamstress friend to make two custom-made hats that honor the pair's Welsh heritage.

When we call for a follow-up, we are delighted to learn that Minnie and Roy minded their manners throughout the party. Sure, they slurped their tea, but that was nothing compared to the rumpus started by the Queen's corgis!

COCO'S TIPS ARF!
DOGGIE DIET ESSENTIALS

IF YOUR DOG IS ANYTHING LIKE THESE CORGIS, KEEPING A SLEEK PHYSIQUE ISN'T EASY. REMEMBER THE FOLLOWING GUIDELINES.

- *No matter how much your dog begs, don't overfeed him!*

- *Exercise is a must. Try this one for the reluntant exerciser: have your pooch lie down on her tummy, then have her get up. Repeat and reward.*

- *Snacks don't always have to be dog treats. Try ice cubes, especially on a hot day.*

before like puppy,
like owner

**DOLLY THE SHEEP SHOULD BE
THE ONE AND ONLY CLONE!**

pooch profile

meet Lily, a two-and-a-half-year-old West Highland terrier, who lives in New York's Upper East Side. A trained therapy dog, Lily frequents hospitals, schools, and nursing centers.

likes Playing with children and being massaged.

dislikes Loud noises, especially ones that come from behind.

the challenge The goal is to let Lily's individual personality shine through without disrupting the harmony between owner and pet.

the solution If Madonna can reinvent herself with a costume change, so can Lily.

lesson learned It doesn't matter what we wear, we're still best friends.

The Look-Alikes

PREPPY PUP DIGS DOWNTOWN STYLE

Lily and her owner have so many things in common: hair color and cut, wardrobe, accessories, even the distinctive swagger in their walk. But Lily is growing up and her owner realizes she deserves a personality and a style to call her own. Coco and I are impressed by her selfless attitude. Can we keep these two-of-a-kind together while sorting out what makes Lily unique?

the back story

Coco and I are familiar with this predicament. In fact, we have received numerous letters and requests to help distinguish dogs from their owners. We've even seen some unfortunate examples of owners and dogs sharing the same mullet-style haircut. Up until now, however, we've never taken on the look-alike challenge, but the warm connection between pet and owner wins us over.

We are determined to keep Lily and her owner connected while accentuating their separate identities. But how? Lily's owner helps steer us in a promising direction when she says, "Lily's much more downtown than I am. I mean, if she were human she'd probably be content to go to clubs and socialize. I like things a bit more mellow." Ah ha! With this information, Coco and I know just what we need to do. "Remember," I speak aloud to Coco,

"opposites do attract." Just because owner and pet are BFF, they don't have to be twins.

Coco and I meet with Lily and her owner at the small neighborhood dog run. At first, Lily is too shy to leave her owner's side (they really are joined at the hip). Coco takes off running down the length of the dog park, barking at Lily to join her. Suddenly, Lily runs to join her at top speed. After frolicking in the grass together for a while, the two return to us, panting and out of breath.

Then I observe Lily as she hops atop a park bench and stares downtown at the city skyline. If I opened the gate to the dog park, would Lily bolt for the bright lights and big city beckoning below? Rather than tempt her with such an option, Coco and I decide to bring downtown up to her.

after tickled pink

LILY LOOKS DELIGHTFUL IN A STYLE THAT'S ALL HER OWN.

the makeover

Every doggie needs to feel like an individual, even within the family pack.

1. Lily's prim and proper Upper East Side 'do needs a redo. We stop off at her usual salon for a trim. The owner hand-strips Lily's hair to encourage the wavy outer coat to grow in. Next he expertly blow-dries her hair and shapes it with pear- and cassis-scented mist (see Resources: Beauty). Finally, he delicately twists some of the curls around her face to get that chrysanthemum-effect prized in Westies.

2. Lily, just like her name, is one very girly dog. We choose pink, pink, and more pink to give her wardrobe that "girls just wanna have fun" style to accentuate her high-spirited, free-loving persona. Where do all the hip pinksters go to accessorize? Hello Kitty boutique shops, of course (see Resources: Fashion and Accessories). Lily doesn't seem to have a problem with flaunting fashion more popularly associated with a cat—at least, not when the cat is as cute and loveable as this Japanese pop icon!

3. Lily sleeps in the same bed with her owner. While this is occasionally acceptable, a pup needs a room of her own, too. Coco and I search online and discover the perfect poppy pink bed: girly and stylish! With a bold, colorful bed like this, Lily will be sure to revel in her privacy.

4. I can't help but remember Lily staring longingly at the cityscape downtown, so I convince a dog-loving friend to take her on weekly field trips south of Fourteenth Street, where they can explore the city's coolest hotspots one by one. This way, Lily's owner can stay within her comfort zone while Lily is free to embark on new adventures.

Lily is smitten with her new look (not to mention her handsome new chaperone) and her owner is happy to see her bloom. We knew all along that their relationship would endure a shift in style.

COCO'S TIPS ARF!
A HEALTHY WHITE COAT

GROOMING A WESTIE REQUIRES A LOT OF TIME AND PATIENCE, BUT IF YOU CHOOSE YOU CAN DO THE WORK YOURSELF.

- *Start when your Westie's still a pup so she gets used to the process.*

- *To hand-strip a Westie, use your left hand to pick up the coat. Use your right hand to strip out only the longest hairs. Only pull the hair in the direction the coat grows.*

- *If you choose this method, do not bathe your pet first. This makes the hair slippery and harder to pull.*

ms. know-it-all

AS THE NEIGHBORHOOD'S FOREMOST FOUR-LEGGED BUSYBODY, RUBY PROUDLY KEEPS TRACK OF THE LOCAL HUBBUB.

pooch profile

meet Ruby, a ten-year-old bichon frisé mix who's excited to explore the world beyond the Garden State.

likes Chasing squirrels and cats . . . oh, and peanut butter.

dislikes The vacuum cleaner!

the challenge Ruby's sensible look works for getting rowdy cats in line, but on the laidback beaches of Waikiki? Wipe out!

the solution A gentle bath, a pedicure, and a casual but pretty outfit are just the thing for Ruby.

lesson learned It's never too late to teach an old dog to hula!

Vacation of a Lifetime

A RETIRED POOCH GETS A NEW LEASH ON LIFE

When Ruby's owner retired to travel, Ruby decided it was time to resign, too. Serving as head of the neighborhood community watch has been exhausting (chasing squirrels and cats is a full-time job), and Ruby is ready for some fun. Coco and I must exchange her work-a-day look for a more relaxed style.

the back story

Ruby is a world-class patroller of cats, postmen, and squirrels. When she's not pacing the sidewalks, she keeps a keen watch over all the local goings-on from her windowsill. After spending the better part of a decade in this demanding routine, Ruby is ready to cast off her watchdog habits and have some fun in the sun. Secretly, Ruby has always yearned to see the world, but keeping up with the local gossip and maintaining a watchful eye on the roaming cats and the unruly squirrels has kept her too dog-tired to travel.

We sit down with Ruby and her owner to discuss their joint travel plans—and Ruby's style makeover to match. We soon discover that although Ruby displays a tail-wagging enthusiasm for world travel, neither she nor her owner have any idea where to begin. Although bold on her home turf, it seems that Ruby is fearful of leaving the comfort zone of her neighborhood.

A mountain getaway is out of the question—too many four-legged critters. Though Ruby has always wanted to go to Barcelona, we quickly eliminate that option as well—far too many *gatos*. Ah, but the beach! Ruby has no issue with seagulls or, for that matter, birds of any sort. At our suggestion of "Hawaii," Ruby runs in circles. But questions arise: How will they get there? Will Ruby have to be stuffed below the cabin with the rest of the luggage? It must be warm and sunny in the islands: how will Ruby deal with the sun and heat? The ocean is another worry: can she drink that salty water?

We promise to address all of these concerns. "We'll make sure you travel in complete comfort—and, of course, in the very best style," we assure the retirees.

after *polynesian princess*

RUBY, LOOKING FRESH AND PRETTY IN HER GRASS SKIRT, ORCHID LEIS, AND SUNGLASSES.

the makeover

"Ruby deserves the vacation of a lifetime," we declare. Here's how Coco and I pull together her trip and her stylish new look.

1. Ruby's owner wants to be sure that Ruby will travel in comfort. With that in mind, we book a window seat for her owner, and select a luxurious Sherpa Houndtooth Paris Pet Carrier for Ruby (see Resources: Fashion and Accessories), specifically designed with travel regulations in mind. We also book Ruby in a pampered pooch suite at her hotel, now de rigueur at many fine hotels.

2. We draft Ruby's "what to pack" list and organize her toiletries (including doggy sunscreen) in matching cosmetic bags. We also create a travel file containing Ruby's most recent certificate of health and immunization records, her medications and vitamins with prescriptions if necessary, and emergency contact information, including her vet's details.

3. A trip to the mall solves all wardrobe dilemmas. To achieve the just-right laidback look Hawaii is known for, we outfit Ruby with the island's main staple: a grass skirt adorned with tropical flowers. Since both retirees have expressed hope of finding a little romance while on their big vacation, we give them matching heart-shaped sunglasses. Look out for love!

4. Ruby adores getting her hair and nails done. An average shedder, she needs only a slight trim followed by a dry shampoo and a nice Shiatsu-style brushing. A classic pedicure refreshes her look.

5. Finally, to make sure Ruby will get the full Waikiki Beach treatment, we surprise her with dinner tickets to a luau, complete with hula lessons.

We know our mission is accomplished when we see photos of Ruby happily relaxing in her hula outfit on a pristine white beach . . . next to a handsome Jack Russell terrier.

COCO'S TIPS
DOGGY TRAVEL

COCO OFFERS THE FOLLOWING POINTERS FOR OWNERS WITH MUTTS ON THE MOVE.

- *Invest in a soft dog carrier with removable wheels. That way you have the option of either rolling or carrying your best friend.*

- *A quick Web search will yield tons of international venues with bow-wow concierges, pet taxis, and doggy room service.*

- *Don't forget to pack a sunscreen specifically for pups labeled SPF 15 or higher (see Resources: Beauty). Apply the sunscreen to hairless areas like the nose, ear tips, and tummy. Dogs with short coats (especially white dogs) should get an all-over application.*

- *Finally, drinking saltwater makes dogs sick, so if you're going to the beach, be sure to bring an adequate supply of fresh, clean water for your dog to drink.*

before *is it snack time yet?*

OTTO HAS NEVER MET A DOUGHNUT HE DIDN'T LIKE.

pooch profile

meet Otto, a four-year-old English bulldog. A stay-at-home couch potato by day and gentleman of leisure by night, Otto has never been one to burn extra calories.

likes Eating, sleeping, and watching television shows with his owner. He also enjoys popping balloons at birthday parties.

dislikes Little white dogs, motorcycles, and vegetables.

the challenge It won't be easy to transform this spud into a stud!

the solution Get Otto on a doggone diet! If he's going to loose weight, this pooch needs less calories and more exercise.

lesson learned A healthier dog is a happier dog!

Worth the Weight

OTTO GOES FROM SPUD TO STUD!

Fighting the battle of the bulge is never an easy feat, but Otto needs to loose some weight. To help him attain a sleeker physique, we'll put this couch potato on a strict diet and challenging exercise regimen. After that, even if Otto indulges in the occasional binge, he'll still inspire admiration in his slenderizing new athletic wear.

the back story

Otto is perfectly content to lounge his days away in front of the television, sneaking food from his owner's plate. Sometimes Otto whines just to get a tiny scrap of leftovers. Sadly, Otto's owner caves in to the bulldog's demands every time and has never reprimanded him for his obnoxious behavior.

At first, Coco and I aren't sure what to do to motivate Otto. Then we think of Tyson, the celebrated skateboarding dog. We know Tyson's mind-boggling moves will get Otto's attention, not only because he's a very talented pooch but also because he's a bulldog, just like Otto.

The usually nonchalant dog appears to be transfixed when I pop Tyson's video into the player. As Tyson skates through various obstacle courses, I can tell that Otto's owner is impressed by the dog's cool moves, too. "See," I say, "that could just as easily be Otto."

At that very moment, Otto leaps from the couch and begins to run (well, jog might be more accurate) around the coffee table. "Whoa," Otto's owner says. "Is he . . . running?" "I think so," I reply.

We watch Otto as he rounds the coffee table again—his third lap. "Go, Otto, go!" I cheer, after which he promptly lies down and falls asleep. When I ask Otto's owner how much Otto weighs, he shrugs his shoulders. We move him to the bathroom scale—to get an approximate reading—and are shocked by the number. After I point out that his buddy's extra weight threatens his longevity, Otto's owner agrees he needs to get the bulldog on a serious diet and exercise routine.

Now that everyone has agreed to the same mission—a slimmer, healthier Otto—it's time to roll up our sleeves and get to work.

after salad, anyone?

OTTO LOOKING SVELTE IN HIS ATHLETIC WEAR.

the makeover

Here's how Coco and I transformed Otto from a lump to a champ.

1. Before we start Otto on his new diet and exercise routine, we consult his veterinarian, who thinks it's an excellent idea for Otto to lose some weight.

2. First, we target the habits behind Otto's weight gain. From our observations, we know that Otto is a beggar. We advise Otto's owner that he needs to break the cycle of addiction. Although it will be difficult, he can no longer offer Otto table scraps and must steel himself against Otto's persistent whining.

3. Next, we take a look at the kind of dog food Otto eats. We soon discover that Otto's owner buys whatever food happens to be on sale. We advise him to choose one high-quality dog food brand—meat, not corn, should be the first ingredient on the label—and stick with it. We also add a daily powdered vitamin supplement to Otto's routine (see Resources: Food and Vitamin Supplements).

4. We record Otto's pre-diet weight (oh, my!) and reduce his daily food ration by one-third, including healthy treats and snacks. After two weeks, we'll weigh Otto again and chart his progress.

5. We hire a fitness expert to devise a simple yet effective doggie exercise routine (see Resources: Training). Designed to prevent boredom and keep Otto moving, the regime consists of daily walks in the park, stick fetching, and an evening jog around the track. We buy Otto a skateboard, too, hoping that he'll take to it like Tyson. Otto, however, simply sniffs it and plops down beside it. Hmmm . . . maybe he'll need some time to warm up to skating.

6. A couple of smart sweat suits allow Otto to move freely and show off his burly physique to the best advantage.

Two weeks later, Otto's owner reports a transformed bulldog: although Otto has only lost only a pound or two, he welcomes his workouts and gobbles up salad greens with gusto! We feel confident that this once-lazy bulldog is on the path to a healthier, happier lifestyle.

COCO'S TIPS
DOGGIE WEIGHT LOSS

WHEN IT COMES TO KEEPING TRIM, COCO KNOWS A THING OR TWO.

- *Consult your veterinarian before putting your dog on a diet.*

- *Make sure your dog is eating a high-protein dog food and has access to fresh water at all times.*

- *Don't give in to begging: table scraps can pack on the pounds and extra pounds can lead to joint problems.*

before
no model ford

**FASHION-CHALLENGED FORD
ENJOYS A ROMP IN THE YARD.**

pooch profile

meet Ford, a black Russian terrier. A rambunctious one-year-old, he is an expert toy and rope shredder.

likes Chewing Guinevere's scratching post, eating catnip, and being sprayed with the water hose.

dislikes Bedtime and having wool blankets pulled over his eyes.

the challenge If Naomi and Tyra can make up, there's no reason why Guinevere and Ford can't live in harmony.

the solution Woo that prickly cat by cleaning up Ford's scruffy looks and rowdy ways.

lesson learned Though friendship may be a challenging pursuit, it's worth the chase.

50   *Shaggy Chic*

Ford and the Pussycat

BEFRIENDING A FINICKY FELINE

Guinevere has never taken kindly to strangers, especially ones of the canine persuasion. After all, she is a finicky feline. When Ford, a large Russian terrier, bounded through her front door last month, Guinevere felt as though she had lost one of her nine lives. The secret to soothing her ruffled coat? When the cat's away, the dog will get a makeover.

the back story

The newest member of Guinevere's household is a sight to be seen. He exemplifies everything Guinevere finds distasteful in dogs. The fact that he arrives, post-adoption, lacking even the most basic grooming tools, wardrobe, or fashion accessories makes Guinevere hiss in disgust. Good-natured to a fault, Ford mistakes Guinevere's battle cry for a friendly hello and greets her with a sloppy lick across the face. The cat's screeching meow is heard by every member of the household. They are in for a difficult transition.

The differences seem to multiply: while Guinevere can spend countless hours grooming herself, Ford rarely cleans himself. Guinevere likes to drape herself in multi-colored strands of ribbon, string, and tinsel. The color-blind Ford has little interest in these shiny materials, although he'll snap at yarn in a manner that Guinevere finds most distressing. There's no way around it: Ford is a dog's dog—simple, lovable, and eager to play.

When Coco and I visit their home, Guinevere has managed to squeeze herself into the crawl space behind the radiator, in an effort to hide from Ford. Ford, however, has spotted her tail and is sitting patiently on the other side, waiting for Guinevere to emerge. I ask the owners how long this standoff has been going on, to which they reply, "Days." Clearly they are concerned Guinevere will never come out.

Coco and I realize that Ford needs more than just a nudge to put his best paw forward. But we have high hopes that we can negotiate a peace settlement between these two.

after l brake for cats

NOW EVEN GUINEVERE HAS TO ADMIT THAT FORD IS THE CAT'S PAJAMAS.

the makeover 🐾

Although Ford is the newcomer, both Guinevere and Ford deserve a chance at happiness in their own home.

1. First, Coco and I take Ford to Chelsea Calico, a renowned animal communicator, which is kind of like a psychic for four-legged creatures (see Resources: Specialists). After spending a soul-searching hour with Ford, Chelsea intuits that Ford sincerely means no harm, but just cannot live up to Guinevere's high standards. He is trying his best to fit in with his new family and doesn't realize that his rowdiness makes Guinevere uncomfortable. She gives Ford some gentle pointers on how to live with Guinevere's prickly persona.

2. We then pay a visit to the doggie salon, where Ford gets a bath—and an impromptu lesson in the art of self-grooming from the resident cat. Hopefully, he'll follow her example and groom himself between bath days, making sure to stretch for hard to reach places, like between his toe pads.

3. Ford's dental hygiene is a major problem. He has been caught more than once eating Guinevere's food and his breath smells, well, a little fishy. The vet cleans his teeth and suggests that his owners give him a daily brushing. The vet also gives the pooch a month's supply of Greenies, a great-tasting dental treat that helps clean teeth, gets rid of plaque and tartar, and eliminates doggie breath (see Resources: Beauty).

4. Coco and I fill Ford's closet with every sort of doggie accoutrement imaginable to encourage good habits and help him feel at home: brushes, an assortment of collars and leashes, biodegradable doggie bags, and a toothbrush and toothpaste.

5. We also stop off at a local boutique that specializes in accessories for cats. Here, we supply Ford with peace offerings for Guinevere: a charming heart-shaped locket and replacements for all the cat toys he's destroyed.

Ford's entrance leaves Guinevere speechless. "Cat got your tongue?" I tease. Although the pair still have to learn to share their home, it looks like a truce has been brokered.

COCO'S TIPS ꞏARF!ꞏ
SECRETS OF PEACEFUL COHABITATION

WHEN A CAT AND DOG WILL BE SHARING A HOUSEHOLD, DON'T UNDERESTIMATE THE POTENTIAL FOR STRIFE.

- *Always supervise their first introduction closely. If a fight threatens, place the animals in separate rooms.*

- *Never use punishment when training dogs and cats to cohabit. Instead, use positive reinforcement to reward them for good behavior.*

- *Make sure cats have plenty of opportunity to stalk and pounce on things other than the dog's tail!*

pooch profile

meet Skyler, a Samoyed. His parents are champion sled dogs.

likes Sledding, playing with stuffed animals, and burying bones.

dislikes Getting his hair brushed and being left alone.

the challenge Get this Samoyed to forget the snowbanks and enjoy the surf.

the solution We'll put Skyler's sweater in the deep freeze and add some sizzle to his style.

lesson learned You don't have to live in an icy climate to be cool.

Where's the Snow?

A SLED DOG HEADS SOUTH

Skyler's family just moved south. Way south: from Siberia to Sarasota, to be precise. It's clear Skyler hasn't acclimated to the warm weather; he's the only pup in Florida wearing a heavy wool sweater. The fashion forecast for this snow cone may seem dreary. Give him a little time to thaw, though, and he'll be chillin' by the beach.

the back story

When Skyler's owner decided to leave Siberia for good, he couldn't possible know that the move to Florida would have such a profound effect on Skyler. Even though Skyler's favorite game is hide-and-seek in the snow, his owner expected Skyler to gladly trade in snow for sand. Boy, was he wrong.

While the rest of the family happily settles into their new digs, Skyler seems restless and uneasy. Although the temperature in Sarasota frequently soars into the nineties, Skyler refuses to let anyone remove his sweater. Skyler's owner is beginning to realize how homesick he is. Will he ever acclimate to his new surroundings?

Time for a little climate control. I take a flight to Florida, where Skyler's family welcomes me into their new home. "It's like an igloo in here," I say, and Skyler's owner

confesses that Skyler bares his teeth if anyone tries to reset the air-conditioner. Skyler's sly way of bringing Siberia to Sarasota? He wonders.

I go to the fridge and offer Skyler some ice cubes. As he cautiously approaches me, his owner quickly pulls the plug on the air-conditioner. (Hey, tricky situations call for tricky solutions.) The temperature begins to rise and Skyler's owner gently coaxes the sweater off the hot dog. Skyler shakes himself out and stretches; he looks liberated. I open some windows and Skyler's nose shoots into the air. Taking in the beachy smells, Skyler knows this is no place like home, but maybe he can grow to accept it. "I'm so proud of you, Skyler!" I say warmly.

We've made it down one slippery slope, now it's time to complete Skyler's warm weather makeover.

after *chillin' in the sun*

SKYLER, STYLIN' IN A TROPICAL SHIRT.

the makeover

Helping Skyler adjust to his new environment will take lots of patience, not to mention creativity.

1. We thought we'd begin by letting Skyler chill out, Siberian style. We take him to the local pup pool for an icy dip. Because of his thick protective coat, we make sure to towel-dry him thoroughly afterward.

2. Skyler's beautiful coat has been hidden by his sweater. We take him to a local groomer, who gives him a dry shampoo and an application of unscented talcum powder. A prolific shedder in the best of circumstances, the stress of the move is causing Skyler to shed profusely. He'll require daily brushing and, as a preventative measure, I recommend Vitacoat Plus to Skyler's owner (see Resources: Food and Vitamin Supplements). This fatty acid supplement keeps pup's coats healthy.

3. Since we know Skyler likes to keep it cool, we'll outfit him with some innovative gear to help him do just that. The Canine Cooler dog bed is a cooling mattress designed to help dogs regulate their temperature (see Resources: Furniture). Fluid-filled and flea-proof, the bed is great for pooches who live in hot climates.

4. We also advise Skyler's owner that the Samoyed needs to drink lots of water, take regular swims, limit his exercise time on particularly hot days, and have sunscreen, preferably SPF 30, applied to his coat.

5. I bet you're wondering about Skyler's beloved sweater, huh? Let's just say we found a new home for that. After a quick visit to a thrift store, we have a whole new wardrobe for Skyler to chill in. Besides being much cooler than his sweater (literally), his tropical shirt screams Sarasota and will help Skyler fit in with the locals.

In fact, the last time we spotted Skyler, he was lounging under the shade of a beach umbrella, a bottle of suntan lotion by his side. Who says Siberians don't know how to have fun?

COCO'S TIPS ARF!

HOT DOG! HELP IS ON THE WAY

TAKE CARE OF YOUR POOCH WHEN TEMPERATURES RISE.

- *Never leave your dog alone in a vehicle! A parked car can become a furnace in no time at all.*

- *Schedule outdoor playtime in the evening, when it's cooler.*

- *Good grooming can stave off warm weather skin problems.*

camera ready

**THE NATURALLY STYLISH LANA LOVES
HAVING HER PICTURE TAKEN.**

pooch profile

meet Lana, a three-year-old pug transplanted from San Francisco. A model pup, she's been in show biz as long as she can remember.

likes Sunbathing, getting her beauty sleep, and nibbling on pieces of grass.

dislikes Bodies of water, including the bathtub. Sharing the spotlight with other dogs.

the challenge It shouldn't be too difficult to transform Lana's runway style to red-carpet sizzle.

the solution We'll show this diva how to dress for success.

lesson learned It doesn't matter if you win or lose; what matters is whether you're stylish at the awards ceremony.

Red-Carpet Debut

LANA, A REAL HEAD-TURNER

Lana's modeling career is already off and running. She even has a few "best in shows" under her patent leather collar. When she's nominated for the prestigious Rover Award, her agent asks us if we'd like to come up with a winning look for the awards ceremony. You bet! We welcome the opportunity to get Lana ready for her red-carpet debut.

the back story

Lana is used to being in the spotlight, posing with fashion icons, and cavorting with creative types. Even though she's comfortable with flashbulbs and media hounds, her agent explains that she's never walked the red carpet. It's a huge opportunity for her, and a style challenge, too.

Not to worry: Coco and I have styled many dog celebrities for similar events. In fact, red-carpet debuts are our stock in trade! Before you think this is going to be a complete breeze, though, we should point out that finding the perfect outfit isn't always easy. There are a lot of components to be considered: the pooch's personality, the color that will best accentuate her features, and a myriad of other design decisions (not to mention what the competition will be wearing). Good thing we're pros and ready to tackle the situation head-on!

Coco and I begin by digging up some details on the award ceremony. Turns out that the competition for this Rover Award is pretty stiff. We decide this situation calls for a little undercover work: we must know what Lana's rivals will be wearing! Luckily, we know where to get the scoop. We visit the finest dog boutiques on Madison Avenue and find out who's dressing whom and who's wearing what. The red-carpet highlights of the Academy Awards pale in comparison to the gowns that are about to make an entrance at this event. We have never seen such star-studded duds.

After our day of detective work, we have a clear vision for Lana and her big debut. We'll make sure she sashays right past the other glamour pooches to claim the prize. Roll out that red carpet, here comes the Rover Award-winning Lana!

after award-winning style

LANA, DRESSED TO THE NINES.

the makeover

Clearly the most talented (not to mention gorgeous) pup in the pack, Lana deserves to win the Rover Award. Time to give her the star treatment.

1. First and foremost, Lana needs her beauty rest before the big event. We outfit an entire bedroom for her, complete with armoire, storage steps, day bed, and toy chest. The Catalina Collection sets the standard for unprecedented luxury (see Resources: Furniture). As soon as she sees the elegant bed, Lana curls up in a tight ball and falls asleep.

2. After Lana is well rested, we take a stroll to an exclusive salon, where the stylish groomer prepares a warm bath. Lana is hesitant but the groomer coaxes her to dip one pad in at a time until she jumps into the tub. The groomer uses a mild no-rinse soap that smells like lavender, and concentrates on making sure low-to-the ground Lana's underside and legs are clean. After a thorough drying and brushing with natural bristles, Lana is ready for her pedicure. The groomer trims Lana's nails and applies Top Performance Nail Sanitizing Spray to reduce the risk of infection from minor nicks and cuts (see Resources: Beauty).

3. Since Lana will be photographed again and again tonight, we want her face to shine. The groomer gently massages Lana's forehead and uses a soft, damp cloth to clean Lana's charming wrinkles and the top of her head. The on-site dentist gives her teeth and tongue a thorough brushing. Divine!

4. Then we unveil the show-stopping dress. Complete with faux fur, dazzling jeweled buttons, an amethyst bracelet, and a chic purse, this pretty-in-pink number is undeniably gorgeous. The color will pop against the red carpet, not to mention Lana's fawn coat, and we are sure the other pooches will be drop-dead envious.

5. Once Lana is dressed, we invite her agent into our studio, where a mock red carpet lines the floor. Lana dazzles us all with her style and confidence in this trial run. We toast to her success before her agent whisks her off in a limo.

It'll come as no surprise that Lana's red-carpet debut ended in triumph. She brought home the Rover Award and we can't help but believe that our glamorous stylings played at least a bit part in her victory.

COCO'S TIPS

RUB-A-DUB PUG

PUG'S REQUIRE SPECIAL TREATMENT AT BATH TIME.

- *Carefully wash the fold that runs down from the eyes beside the nose. Lift the over-nose wrinkle and carefully wash inside this fold.*

- *After washing the rest of the pug, dry thoroughly with an absorbent towel.*

- *Powder may be used, but never on the over-nose wrinkle, where it might get trapped.*

before jailbird

RALPH DOESN'T SEEM TO UNDERSTAND THAT THE KENNEL IS NOT A PUNISHMENT.

pooch profile

meet Ralph, an eleven-year-old terrier mix, born and raised on Staten Island.

likes Rolling in the grass, walking in the woods, and swimming.

dislikes Getting groomed and having his paws touched.

the challenge Ralph may *feel* like a felon but he doesn't need to *look* like he's been working on a chain gang.

the solution Take advantage of Ralph's "jail time" to rehabilitate his disheveled look.

lesson learned A manicure and a haircut can do wonders for a guilty conscience.

Free at Last

THIS LITTLE DOGGIE IS SCRUFFY NO MORE

When Ralph's owners go on a business trip, they must leave the dog at the kennel for a week. Confused by the change in environment, Ralph enters his crate as though it's a jail sentence, his tail between his legs. Coco and I check in on the pooch, and decide to make good use of his "jail time" by rehabilitating his scruffy look.

the back story

Ralph watches as his owners pack their suitcases for their business trip, thinking that he gets to go along. But after being fed a very special dinner of steak tips and baby carrots, he has a hunch that he isn't going on the trip after all.

That night, Ralph's owners hear him growling in his sleep and wonder if he's having nightmares about being left behind, and about what he could possibly have done to deserve it. Is he being reprimanded for chasing Felix up the oak tree last week? Do his owners hate him because he took a dip in the neighbor's pool? How about the time he rolled in mud and slept on the new carpet? Oh, the possibilities are endless. Ralph tosses and turns.

The next morning, the suitcases are in the trunk, the car is running, and Ralph's owners lovingly offer him his favorite leash. Trying to demonstrate what a good dog he

can be, Ralph obliges and carries the leash in his mouth to the backseat of the car. Despite his obedience, he fears he's going to be locked up anyway.

Ralph's worst-case scenario becomes reality when they enter the kennel. His owners leave him with an attendant, and he watches with wistful eyes as they walk out the door. Ralph is uncomfortable in his new surroundings. There are lots toys and other dogs to play with, but where are his owners? He wants to play with them. Bedtime is lonely. There is no one to snuggle up with and no one to give him a belly rub. He will have a lot of time for reflection while he is serving his sentence.

Coco and I visit Ralph in the kennel to reassure him that his owners aren't punishing him. I tell him: "There's nothing wrong with your behavior, Ralph, but you look as unkempt as a convict. Time for a makeover!"

after free as a bird

AN ANGELIC-LOOKING RALPH ENJOYS HIS LIBERATION FROM THE KENNEL.

the makeover 🐾

After reminding Ralph that he'll be reunited with his owners soon, we spruce him up for the day he'll be sprung.

1. To help put Ralph's misplaced guilt to rest, we escort him to a portion of the kennel he's never visited: the swimming pool. We know he loves to swim and hope a dip in the pool will make him feel like the kennel is a place to have fun while his owners just happen to be away for a few days. Although we aren't certain Ralph gets the message, he definitely enjoys his swim!

2. Ralph is still feeling a little guilty, so he is amenable to grooming. Fortunately, this kennel has an in-house salon. First, this already wet dog gets a bath. The groomer uses Perfect Coat White Pearl shampoo, a gentle whitening shampoo that makes his coat sparkle (see Resources: Beauty). A terrier mix like Ralph only needs a bath a few times a year (or whenever he rolls in the mud).

3. After his coat is dry, the groomer gives this still scruffy dog a brushing. Since he's a terrier mix, his hair is long, wiry, and weatherproof, not close-lying like many of his terrier relatives. A gentle but thorough brushing painlessly removes tangles and excess hair. Finally, Ralph gets what his groomer calls "a heavy trim up": a tidy-up of his long body hair, a shave in the rear section, and a serious trimming of the hair around his eyes and ears. What a transformation!

4. We tell Ralph his owners will definitely forgive any wrongdoings if they're greeted with a sparkling grin that matches his coat. So, Ralph allows the groomer to brush and polish his teeth without a fuss. His makeover complete, Ralph is ready for hugs and kisses galore.

Before Ralph's owners arrive, we take him on a walk to reacquaint him with the great outdoors. With leash in mouth, and tail held high, he rambles around the kennel grounds, possibly thinking that serving time hasn't been so bad after all!

COCO'S TIPS ARF!
KENNEL CONSIDERATIONS

HERE'S HOW TO FIND A KENNEL WORTHY OF YOUR POOCH.

- *Ask other pet owners for kennel recommendations. Before you make a reservation, pay the kennel a visit and ask to be shown around.*

- *Be sure that the kennel is properly licensed and trust your first impressions. If the kennel doesn't look clean or the animals look unhappy, it's not the right place for your precious pooch.*

before daydreamers

POLLY AND UNDERDOG, DREAMING OF ADVENTURE-FILLED DAYS.

pooch profile

meet Feisty Polly Purebred, a one-and-a-half-year-old buckethead beagle, and stubborn Underdog, a two-year-old French basset hound.

likes Polly likes to snuggle under the blankets and receive constant attention. Underdog likes to sleep by himself and howl at the moon.

dislikes They both dislike being separated from each other.

the challenge Coco and I are determined to add a dash of dreamlike adventure to Polly and Underdog's mundane lives.

the solution By the time our makeover is complete, Polly and Underdog will be the heroes of their own reality.

lesson learned Dreams really can come true!

Fulfilling a Fantasy

POLLY AND UNDERDOG SHARE A DREAM

Bored with their mundane, day-to-day routine, the inseparable Polly and Underdog indulge in extraordinary daydreams. It's no coincidence that these pups begin to embody the superhero qualities of their legendary namesakes, the stars of the popular cartoon *The Underdog Show*. Coco and I analyze their drowsy whimpers and eyelid flutters to unlock the mysteries of their heroic dream lives . . .

the back story

It really is a dog's life for Polly and Underdog. Their humdrum suburban existence pales in comparison with that of their working dog friends. They don't stand guard at the firehouse or sniff out a crime scene. They don't visit hospitals or nursing centers. They don't even protect the neighborhood from unwelcome stray cats. Instead, they are housebound. Their stay-at-home job requires only that they bestow lots of affection upon their owners and anyone else who's invited into their home. Sure, they're generously compensated with gourmet foods and treats galore but, man, are they bored. Who knew that a life of relaxation could be so unfulfilling?

Polly and Underdog spend the majority of their days sleeping in front of the television. Their owner, a stay-at-home dad, likes to keep the television on as background noise while he cleans up the house or prepares for dinner. As a consequence, Polly and Underdog are probably more up-to-date with the latest soap opera melodramas and action-packed cartoons than their owners. "It's not surprising that these pups have wild dreams," I explain to Coco. "They probably confuse their lives with the lives of the television characters they watch." Then *The Underdog Show*, starring Underdog and ace reporter Polly Purebred, comes on the screen, and we realize what a fitting alternative reality it is for our action-adventure-challenged pups.

It seems even pampered pups like Polly and Underdog have unfulfilled fantasies. Coco and I can no longer look the other way while their dreams go unanswered. We boldly decide to go where no stylists have gone before and give this unassuming duo some superpowers to get them through their tedious days. Onward and upward!

after up, up, and away!

THE CANINE SUPERHEROES, NO LONGER INCOGNITO.

the makeover

It doesn't take superpowers to fulfill a fantasy. With a little imagination, we know Polly and Underdog's daydreams will take flight.

1. In order to assume their fantasy roles, this rather un-dynamic duo needs to get into shape. We put the previously lethargic dogs on an exercise regime that includes lots of running and jumping. Like the cartoon characters they'll exemplify, Polly and Underdog will need to build their strength. We put them on Mighty-Vites (see Resources: Food and Vitamin Supplements), a daily vitamin supplement that will keep them fortified when they don't have time to eat right.

2. Next, we enroll the pair in search and rescue training (see Resources: Training). Of course, certification would be a lengthy process, but this introductory class covers the basics—just enough information to give Polly and Underdog the foundations of heroism.

3. Wherever superheroes are busy saving the world, photo ops abound. In order to get these soon-to-be superheroes looking spiffy, they need a good grooming. Polly is an average shedder, unlike Underdog, who sheds constantly. However, since they are both smooth-haired, we use a firm bristle brush to clean up their coats. (We can't have superheroes shedding up a storm!) Beagles and bassets should only be bathed when absolutely necessary. So, a good wipe-down with a damp, coarse cloth and mild soap are sufficient. We finish with a thorough ear and eye cleaning for both.

4. Finally, we take a trip to Wiggle-n-Waggle (see Resources: Fashion and Accessories) for an appropriate wardrobe. After some fittings and custom tailoring, Polly and Underdog are ready to save the planet . . . or at least come in first place at the annual neighborhood Halloween costume contest.

As we drive home from the store in my car, Polly puts her head out one window and Underdog claims the other. With the wind whipping their big ears and ruffling their brightly colored capes, these superdogs look ready for action. Who knows? Maybe they'll join forces with their working dog friends to form a whole league of Canine Superfriends.

COCO'S TIPS
EVEN SUPERHEROES GET DOG-TIRED

HERE'S HOW TO KEEP YOUR DOG'S ENERGY HIGH.

- *Keep your pup hydrated at all times. Folding water bowls by Ruff Wear (see Resources: Fashion and Accessories) are great when you and your dog are on the run.*

- *Consider a daily multi-vitamin for your pup to help keep his immune system strong.*

- *Ear infections will tap your dog's energy: clean his ears thoroughly with a cotton swab to avoid problems.*

before ever alert

MAX'S DAYS ARE SOMETIMES MONOTONOUS, BUT HE NEVER LETS DOWN HIS GUARD.

pooch profile

meet Max, a two-year-old German shepherd. Strong in spirit, body, and mind, he will do anything to protect his family.

likes His around-the-clock job, barking at his owner's red motorcycle, running through autumn leaves, and puppies of all shapes and sizes.

dislikes Loud noises and squeaky doors . . . scary!

the challenge This humble, unsung hero needs some attention thrown his way.

the solution We'll give Max the royal treatment, so there's no doubt in his mind how much his faithful service is appreciated.

lesson learned Loyalty and hard work will be rewarded!

King of the Castle

A VALIANT HERO IS CROWNED

Max is the leader of his pack. A security dog in training, he protects his family from mailbox invasions, speeding vehicles, and the numerous strangers who ring the doorbell. Gentle, lovable Max consistently demonstrates his devotion to his family. In return, they want to honor his service by crowning him king of the castle.

the back story

Both of Max's biological brothers were trained by the local police department. Someday, Max will join them in the family security business. But for now, his human family needs him to pay close attention to what goes on in and around their home, and he takes his responsibilities seriously. In fact, this German shepherd is one of the best around-the-clock security guards in the neighborhood, reassuring not only his family but everyone on the block that they can confidently leave their houses during the day and sleep soundly at night.

The dramatic events of one rainy afternoon only reinforced this perception. The mail arrived intact that day, so Max was free to take an afternoon nap. His sleep was soon disturbed by a crash he first wrote off as thunder. On closer observation, Max discovered a trespasser in his backyard, carrying an empty duffle bag. The stranger had knocked over some trash cans that lined the family's deck.

Always quick to react, Max dashed through the back door and down the deck stairs, deftly cornering the intruder. He barked and growled menacingly, letting neighbors far and wide know that someone other than the postman was on his land. It didn't take long for the nextdoor neighbors to call the police, and soon the burglar was apprehended, all courtesy of Max.

The local police department praised Max for his good work, and the neighbors sent special treats and toys to show their gratitude. Max even got his picture in the newspaper. He is a recognized community hero, but his family wants to be sure that he understands how much *they* appreciate his courage, not just during the attempted robbery but every single day. Can Coco and I come up with a reward to honor his steadfast service?

after the royal treatment

HOME WILL ALWAYS BE A SAFE HAVEN UNDER MAX'S REIGN.

the makeover

What can we possibly do for a dog that gives every day his all, except treat him like the hero he is? Forget the five-star treatment, this canine is a king among men and deserves to be treated as such!

1. Since Max is always on the job, patrolling his home and guarding its residents, we think he deserves to forget about work, at least for one day. We send him to a doggie daycare center in upstate New York that offers plenty of open space—and companions—for Max to run free. A pet chaffeur service (see Resources: Travel) transports him both ways in style.

2. Max needs to look sharp for the evening festivities we've planned. We decide he'll enjoy being pampered by his family in the comfort of his own home. German shepherds don't need to be bathed more than once a month, but since Max has been too busy for such indulgences, his mistress gives him a warm, gentle bath in the backyard that helps him to loosen up and unwind. Forget towel drying: Max chooses to dry himself off in some fresh clean grass.

3. Next his master brushes him with his coat-grooming rake, a process that makes Max moan in pleasure. Although Max's coat is shiny and healthy, regular grooming will maintain his top coat between baths and remove loose hairs from his undercoat.

4. We send Max to the vet for a dental exam and thorough cleaning, where he receives praise for his strong teeth and jaws. We also ask the vet to clean Max's ears and trim his nails. Running in the grass, like walking on pavement, isn't a natural nail file.

5. It's time to crown the king! We've gathered everyone—family, friends, neighbors, and even the local police—in Max's backyard to witness his coronation. After a short but sincere speech thanking Max for his loyalty and hard work, Max's master wraps a handsome cape around his shoulders and his mistress places a crown on his head. Thank you, Max, for a job well done!

Has all the fanfare gone to Max's head? Not in the least: Max continues to perform his daily responsibilities with zest, only now, he wears a crown.

COCO'S TIPS — ARF!
HERO WORSHIP

WANT TO RETURN YOUR FAITHFUL POOCH'S LOVE AND DEVOTION? HERE'S HOW.

- *Surprise him with homemade foods, such as those made by Trudy's Homemade (see Resources: Food and Vitamin Supplements).*

- *Commission a painting or photograph of your pup. Many artists create charming portraits of beloved pets (see Resources: Artwork and Photography).*

before
the neighborhood
favorite

WHEN HE ISN'T BEGGING FOR
TREATS, REMY SERENADES HIS
NEIGHBORS FROM HIS BACK PORCH.

pooch profile

meet Remy Marley, an American Eskimo/sheltie mix and howler of courtyard country tunes.

likes Baby carrots, cruising in his owner's Jeep, and, of course, country music.

dislikes The hair dryer, Swiss cheese, and thunder.

the challenge This pooch deserves to be a country music sensation.

the solution We'll take Remy's singing off his porch and onto a stage.

lesson learned If you have a song in your heart, share it!

The Country Crooner

A HONKY-TONK DOG TAKES TO THE STAGE

Since he was a pup, this dog has always loved to howl along to the stereo. Although his name is Remy Marley, ironically enough, his favorite music is country, not Jamaican reggae. Play a little Garth Brooks or Willie Nelson and listen to Remy yowl. A steel guitar sends him over the moon! We think it's time to outfit this country crooner with a guitar of his own to twang.

the back story

On the threshold of his twelfth birthday, Remy is the most popular dog in his apartment complex, not only for his melodic prowess but also because he magically appears whenever neighbors need to "unpack" their groceries. He always volunteers to put the goodies away . . . in his tummy.

When Remy isn't begging for supermarket goodies, he's listening for sounds of banjos and washboards or the plucking of guitars. On those warm summer nights when apartment doors remain wide open, Remy can be heard howling to whatever country music happens to be playing in the complex at the time. He has serenaded many a terrace and harmonized with countless shower soloists.

Not exactly a country boy, Remy was born and raised in suburban New Jersey. So how did he come to embrace the sounds of country music? "It all started when he was a puppy and my mother played Johnny Cash records whenever she babysat for him. He howled along to every song," explains his owner. "Then my husband let him strum his guitar with his paws." That's how country stars are born, all right, at least in Hollywood movies.

Remy's owner hopes to encourage him to share his country music stylings with a larger audience. "The neighbors love hearing him croon and my mom is so proud that he shares her taste in music," his owner says. What better way to celebrate Remy's twelfth birthday than with a genuine hoedown, where he can perform for friends and family? We'll turn the courtyard into a barnyard and two-step the night away.

after *move over garth*

A COUNTRY STAR IS BORN.

the makeover

If Remy is going to sing like a cowboy, then he should look like one, too. Let's mosey on down to the makeover session.

1. Remy's owner wants to polish up his appearance for his birthday hoedown. Eskimo sheltie mixes like Remy have a double coat of hair that insulates against the heat and cold. So, brushing is the most important part of Remy's grooming. At least once a week, his owner should brush thoroughly from the skin outward to control shedding and keep the coat and skin healthy. Remy has been trained to lie on his side during grooming, which makes brushing a lot easier for his owner.

2. We take Remy to the local groomer for a waterless bath that will help control his static electricity. She lightly mists his coat with Self Rinse Plus, a waterless shampoo that conditions the coat, removes dirt, and keeps static electricity from forming (see Resources: Beauty).

3. When we hear the sound of Remy's nails scraping across the floor, we know that it's time for a nail clipping. The groomer uses a RESCO nail trimmer and keeps Quickstop Powder on hand in case he accidentally cuts too short (see Resources: Beauty).

4. As promised, we bring Remy his very own training guitar. It is a bit smaller than a regular guitar, and we outfit it with steel strings since we want them to hold up to Remy's rough ways. Even if Remy can't play chords on the guitar, he'll still have fun randomly plucking (or biting) the strings. A bandana around his neck and a sheltie-sized cowboy hat complete Remy's look. Let the two-stepping begin!

Everybody raved about the Southern dishes we served at the hoedown. (Remy was particularly fond of the fried catfish.) But the true star of the party was Remy. As if on cue, Remy howled along to a Johnny Cash favorite, "Dirty Old Egg Sucking Dog," and had everyone in stitches. His performance earned him a new nickname, Honky-Tonk Remy, and an invitation to croon at the neighborhood's next block party.

COCO'S TIPS ARF!
DON'T BE SINGING THE SCRUFFY DOG BLUES

LONG-HAIRED DOGS NEED DAILY ATTENTION. HERE'S HOW TO KEEP THEM LOOKING TRIM.

- *Remove tangles with a slicker brush daily, gently teasing out any matted areas.*

- *Once your dog is tangle free, brush his coat with a bristle brush.*

- *To help prevent matting, periodically trim the hair between the pads of his paws.*

before **mama bella**

A DUTIFUL MOM, LADY BELLA HAS SPENT THE LAST MONTH RAISING THREE PUPPIES.

pooch profile

meet Lady Bella, a four-year-old dachshund and proud mother of three.

likes Curling up by the fireplace, playing in the backyard sprinkler, nipping the heels of strangers, and sleeping on pillows.

dislikes Snow, skateboards, and her pink collar.

the challenge It's time to restore some pep in this tuckered-out pooch.

the solution There's nothing that a trip to the spa and a night off can't fix.

lesson learned Every day should be Mother's Day!

Baby on Board

THREE-DOG NIGHT AND DAY

Lady Bella gave birth to triplets last month. She's delighted with her brood, but dog-tired of nursing. Her owners say she is clearly devoted to the three pups, but they're worried that the newborns are running her ragged. We know just what this mama needs: a little pampering herself!

the back story

Because she's such a good-natured dog, Lady Bella's owners decided to breed her. The day she gave birth to triplets was cause for much celebration. The puppies were so irresistible, Lady Bella's owners decided to keep them. This is great news for Lady Bella, except it means that her puppy-raising tasks will continue, even after her brood is weaned. One more reason to give this hardworking pooch a well-deserved respite!

Raising the triplets has been an around-the-clock job for Lady Bella. There's hasn't even been a moment's pause to give them names—beyond Puppies One, Two, and Three, that is. When the triplets wake up in the morning, they wobble into their play area where chaos ensues, with one pup chasing the tails of the other two. Then they toddle to retrieve their teeny toys, which are scattered across the carpet, at which point the yelping begins . . . and continues . . . and continues. Drowsy but

devoted, Lady Bella supervises the whole production, checking out the scene to make sure nothing's been broken or soiled. Then it's breakfast time. The pups crowd around their mom, who must make sure each of them gets enough to eat.

Lady Bella's owners want to be sure that the new mother gets the appreciation she deserves—and a break from her puppy-rearing responsibilities. Lady Bella never complained when her pregnant belly dragged on the kitchen floor or when the triplets cried all night every night for weeks after they were born. "She's so stoic!" her owners exclaim. "That's why it's so important for us to give back to her. Her three little pups have brought so much joy to our household."

Coco and I promise to give Lady Bella a day to remember—minus the triplets.

after mama mia!

LADY BELLA, LOOKING PRETTY IN PINK AFTER HER DAY AT THE SPA.

the makeover 🐾

Time to treat this pooch to an indulgent day of complete relaxation! We'll call it the New Mama Makeover.

1. Lady Bella definitely deserves a nice massage. Her muscles have been working overtime, and lying on her side while nursing has been hard on her back. Our doggie massage specialist demonstrates basic techniques her owners can use to give the tired mom a daily massage. First, she rubs a small amount of body oil (she recommends unscented Neutragena) into her hands, and starting at the top of Lady Bella's spine, slowly strokes the length of the dachshund's back, repeating until the dog sighs contentedly.

2. Since we know that Lady Bella loves to curl up by the fire, we treat her to her very own orthopedic heat and wellness bed (see Resources: Furniture). Usually used for older or incredibly athletic dogs, we decided that motherhood can make a pooch feel like she's simultaneously completed a marathon and fast-forwarded the aging process.

3. We also stock the pantry with plenty of healthy, high-energy foods to help Lady Bella get through the day. It's especially important for a nursing mom to eat nutritiously. Organic and high-protein foods are best for a dog who's feeding a litter of little ones.

4. After a rejuvenating day at the spa, we slip Lady Bella into this pretty hand-knit sweater, especially designed for daschunds, from Barkus Pet Boutique (see Resources: Fashion and Accessories). Pink is clearly her color!

5. As a parting gift to the new mom, we supply her owners with Just Born Milk Replacer for Puppies (see Resources: Food and Vitamin Supplements). This formula closely matches mother's milk and can be used in a pinch—say, when mom is out for a much-needed day at the spa.

We consider our mission accomplished when we see Lady Bella rejoin her pups. Although the triplets are as yippy and demanding as ever, she seems thoroughly rejuvenated and up to the task.

COCO'S TIPS
NEW MAMA RESCUE

IF YOUR DOG BECOMES A MOTHER, SHE'LL NEED SOME EXTRA PAMPERING TO STAY HEALTHY AND HAPPY.

- *New moms should eat a diet rich in protein and vitamins, especially when nursing. (Think lean meats.) Ask your vet for recommendations or try Blue for Dogs, a holistic dog food (see Resources: Food and Vitamin Supplements).*

- *Massage your dog. She will thank you, especially if she's a new mother. Just be sure to select massage oil that is unscented and non-toxic, as pooches tend to lick it.*

pooch profile

meet Atticus Lance Thoreau, better known as Lance, an eight-year-old Airedale terrier and street-smart trickster.

likes Eating, playing outside, teasing neighborhood cats, and chasing bicycles.

dislikes Being touched behind the ears and the sound of the lawn mower.

the challenge This bad boy has got to learn a little respect.

the solution Get ready for the first day of obedience school, Lance!

lesson learned Leave monkey business to the monkeys.

The Graduate

ACING THE SCHOOL OF HARD KNOCKS

Lance gets into more trouble in one week than most pups do in a lifetime. His trail of devilish antics has strained his relationship with his owners, the neighbors, the local fire department, and all the cats within a five-block radius. Once he receives his diploma from obedience school, everyone will breathe a sigh of relief.

the back story

Lance excels at Houdini-like escapes from his leash and loves to chase children's bicycles up and down the avenue—an act that doesn't exactly endear him to their parents. Firemen are called so frequently to rescue cats he has chased up trees that the calls have become a kind of hazing ritual for new firemen. "You got Lanced!" they joke with one another after coaxing a tabby from a roof.

"Lance was such a well-behaved puppy that we never considered sending him to school. But then, something changed—I have no idea what—and he just started acting like a hooligan," explains his master. He's also become a master of manipulation. "He'll pull some outrageous stunt then cuddle up to you, expecting instant forgiveness," his master adds. "And because he's a charmer, he'll usually get it, too."

A few months ago, Lance's owners decided it was time to lay down the law. They established a rigorous course of home schooling for Lance, including daily lessons in how to walk on a leash, heel, stay, and lie down, but Lance continued to act out. Soon, his owners waved the white flag and Lance resumed his mischievous ways. Once again, the cats in the neighborhood are being driven to the rooftops and children avoid riding their bikes past Lance's home. He is getting a very bad rep, indeed! Lance's owners are at their wits' end when they call us to see if we can help get their unruly Airedale back on course.

When Coco and I stop by for a visit, we find Lance toppling the cookie jar. "Lance, no!" I shout. He simply looks at me for two seconds then resumes his criminal behavior, eating as many cookies as he can swipe into his large mouth. "Okay, Lance, we've had enough of your tomfoolery," I say. "You're going to school!"

after the proud graduate

LANCE, LOOKING DISTINGUISHED WITH HIS CAP AND DIPLOMA.

the makeover

Here's hoping we can help Lance embrace the straight and narrow and get his life in order.

1. Lance needs a full-blown behavior makeover. Since Lance is more than a little behind in his training, we decide to hire a tutor to reinforce what he learns in obedience school (see Resources: Training). Lance's owners will also benefit from the extra help. The home tutor will teach them how to manage special situations that come up at home, so they'll know how to effectively discipline Lance the next time he heads for the cookie jar or chases a child on a bicycle.

2. We explain to Lance's owners that successful obedience training is as reliant on the owners' behavior as it is upon the dog's. The obedience school trainers work with them to create a consistent repertoire of commands they both must follow. Slowly, the basic commands that Lance has been ignoring for so long began to make sense. We are all amazed to see the once rambunctious dog follow commands like sit, down, and stay—orders that he used to blithely ignore.

3. A new cookie jar sits next to the old one on Lance's kitchen counter (a gift from Lance's tutor), except this one holds dog treats. Although we don't anticipate any more cookie jar raids, his tutor wants to be sure there will always be a stash of healthy treats to reward Lance's good behavior.

4. We firmly believe that a well-groomed Lance will be a better-behaved Lance. Since obedience school graduation is right around the corner, we make an appointment with a groomer to spiff up Lance's look before the ceremony. Because Lance's family brushes him daily, Lance only needs to be "plucked," a method of getting rid of excessive hair in short woolly coats. He also needs to have his teeth brushed, a ritual that used be an impossible challenge, now made manageable because Lance is a trained dog.

Although Lance wasn't first in his graduating class, you'd think he was valedictorian. When it was time to receive his diploma, the smartly groomed Lance held his head high and heeled beside his master, who had tears in his eyes.

COCO'S TIPS *ARF!*

DOGGIE DENTAL HEALTH

HERE'S HOW TO GET YOUR POOCH READY FOR HIS CLOSE-UP.

- *Brush your dog's teeth at least twice a week with a pet toothpaste (see Resources: Beauty) and a toothbrush with soft bristles. Fingertip rubber brushes work well, too.*

- *Regular professional cleaning by your vet is also a must. A dog's teeth are prone to plaque buildup, periodontal disease, and occasional cavities.*

- *Never use human toothpaste or mouthwash on a pet.*

before baby steps

DA VINCI IS SO ADORABLE, WHO WOULD WANT HIM TO GROW UP?

pooch profile

meet Infant Da Vinci, Chinese Shar-pei, from Somerset, New Jersey.

likes Riding in the car, ice cubes, and getting massaged.

dislikes Bitter apples, his leash, and being patted on the head.

the challenge It's time to get housebroken.

the solution Coco and I teach Da Vinci to make his first baby steps . . . toward a wee-wee pad!

lesson learned Growing up comes with its rewards.

Grow Up

WHAT A BABY!

Some puppies never want to grow up. Or is it their owners who are reluctant to see them leave puppyhood behind? Probably both, we suppose. Da Vinci's owners are guilty as charged, and admit they've been slow to housebreak him. Some positive reinforcement and encouragement are all Da Vinci needs to grow from infant to potty-trained toddler.

the back story

Da Vinci is an impressive moniker for a wrinkly little puppy who looks like he's wearing a pair of slouchy socks, but, like the celebrated artist, he is colorful (apricot to be precise), bright, and inventive. Instead of painting, Da Vinci loves to chew—anything and everything. You might even consider chewing his art form.

Besides his tendency to treat the couch as though it were a chew toy, Da Vinci has an even bigger problem: he hasn't mastered the rules of potty training and occasionally has accidents throughout the house. His owners have scattered wee-wee pads where ever they can think to put them. Without fail, Da Vinci chooses a spot without a pad. "We think he's practicing his signature," his mistress jokes. Knowing that it's high time this puppy gets housebroken, his owners ask if we can lend a hand.

Coco hasn't been a puppy in many years (of course, I would never be so gauche as to reveal her age), and I'd forgotten what to do to house train pups. I decide to call in some experts to help us lay down new rules for the household. When we ask Da Vinci's owners if they have a crate, they respond in unison, "No!" They don't like the idea of locking up Da Vinci, even if just for a few minutes. I ask to see the dog's bed and his owners stare at me blankly. "He sleeps with us," they explain. Clearly, the owners need some new house rules, too.

When it comes to house training, Coco and I will have to come up with a gentle strategy for this wrinkly pup—and for his owners, who clearly love him very much.

after *portrait of an artist*

DA VINCI MASTERS POTTY-TRAINING ETIQUETTE.

the makeover 🐾

Even wrinkle-pup Da Vinci knows it's time to grow up.

1. First comes the potty training. Our team of experts advises on the best methods for house training, starting with the wee-wee pads (see Resources: Training). Though Da Vinci's owners have laid out plenty of pads, they need to increase their words of encouragement so their pup will begin to associate praise with using the wee-wee pad. Whenever Da Vinci's owners see him moving into his "pre-potty pattern" (walking in circles and sniffing the floor), now they pick him up and carry him to the wee-wee pad. Once the job is done, they lavish him with praise. (See, we told you Da Vinci's a smart dog!)

2. Once Da Vinci has mastered the wee-wee pads, our experts begin to move the pads closer and closer to the front door. Soon he is comfortable using those pads, so the next time he starts sniffing the floor and roaming in circles, our experts lead him outside and onto the lawn. It takes some trial and error, but soon Da Vinci masters this routine as well. He is fully housetrained: no on can call him a baby now!

3. Next, we must curb Da Vinci's persistent chewing habits . . . or risk an entire household filled with the dog's "sculptures." With the owners' permission, we apply Bitter Apple spray (see Resources: Training) to the couch. This nontoxic spray won't stain the upholstery, but it's bitter scent discourages dogs from biting and chewing. We test it on Da Vinci, who takes one whiff and recoils.

4. Next comes a dog bed for this pooch. We select a plush, hopefully irresistible bed that's just the right size for the Shar-pei and set it next to his owners' bed. Since they've already allowed Da Vinci to sleep with them, they have to undo his babyish habits. Our experts advise them to use the verbal cue, "Go to your bed," and to reward the pup with a small treat every time he follows these instructions. Although the new bed causes some separation anxiety for both pup and owners, Da Vinci's master admits that their bed was pretty cramped with a dog plopped right between them.

When we check in on Da Vinci's progress, we are delighted to hear that the entire family has adjusted to the new house rules. Congratulations, Da Vinci, you're a big boy now!

COCO'S TIPS ARF!
CLEANING A WRINKLY POOCH

SHAR-PEIS HAVE SPECIAL GROOMING REQUIREMENTS.

- *To clean a Shar-pei's skin, simply lift up each fold and clean underneath with a soft towel. Otherwise, moisture and dirt will collect in the folds, causing an uncomfortable, even moldy rash.*

- *Since their ear canals are so short, Shar-peis are prone to ear infections. Every so often, clean their ears gently with a cotton swab.*

Meet the Models

BELLA AND JASPER
Always willing to share their toys, Bella and Jasper draw the line at sharing treats.

DA VINCI
Da Vinci marches to his own tune. He refuses to sit on his hind legs and prefers, instead, to sit on his rump with his legs spread to each side.

FORD
There's no need for a paper shredder when Ford's around.

HARLEY
When he wants attention, Harley puts some spring in his step. He can jump five feet and three inches—the same height as his owner.

JOEY
If there's one thing Joey can't stand, it's the little black poodle that lives down the block.

LADY BELLA
A model mom, Lady Bella is the belle of the ball to her young charges.

LANA
Like most dogs, Lana would rather lounge naked all day in the sun than wear a dress.

**LANCE
(LANCE ATTICUS THOREAU)**
Lance's full name is a mouthful! His middle name is based on his owner's favorite character from *To Kill a Mockingbird*.

LILY
A total tomboy, Lily wouldn't be caught dead in a dress.

MAX
Max is so well-trained you can put steak in front of his nose and he won't touch it till you give the okay.

90   *Shaggy Chic*

MAXINE
This loveable pooch has the uncanny habit of blocking the TV during the most exciting part of a movie.

MINNIE AND ROY
These rascally twins have been known to cart off poppyseed bagels when no one's looking.

OLIVER
Even though he's full-grown, Oliver insists on being held like a baby.

OTTO
After completing an intensive diet, Otto never wants to see another salad again.

PEBBLES
Pebbles loves to eat her aunt's spaghetti right out of the serving bowl.

POLLY
This pup is a good-time girl, always ready for playtime.

RALPH
Ralph can hold his leash in his mouth and walk himself!

REMY
Remy been known to obsessively bounce a tennis ball on his nose for hours.

RUBY
When no one's looking, Ruby eats sand at the beach.

SKYLER
You'd think this pooch was born in water. He adores swimming and diving.

TROOPER
There's nothing Trooper enjoys more than a ride in his red wagon.

UNDERDOG
Whenever he has a spare moment (and he has *a lot* of spare moments) Underdog rests his bones.

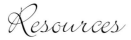

Resources

ARTWORK AND PHOTOGRAPHY

ARTISTS AND STUDIOS
Art Paw
214-321-1150
www.artpaw.com

Amanda Jones
877-251-2390
www.amandajones.com

Petography by Jim Dratfield
1-800-738-6472
www.petography.com

Nikki Solone
916-457-7152
www.petpawtraits.com

Martha Szabo
www.marthaszabo.com

Virginia Wilson
207-233-2580
www.gooddogportraits.com

BEAUTY

SALONS
Best Friends Pet Resort & Salon
www.bestfriendpetcare.com

Find a Groomer
www.findagroomer.com

Pet Groomer
www.petgroomer.com

PETCO Grooming Salon
www.petco.com

PRODUCTS AND STORES
Note: All of the beauty products below can be found at most pet stores. See Store Directory for contact information.

Nail Care
Color Paw
Pretentious Pooch
443.524.7777
www.pretentious pooch.com

Kwik Stop Styptic Powders, Gel, and Pads with Benzocaine and Top Performance Nail Sanitation Spray
Arcata Pet Supplies
800.822.9085
www.arcatapet.com

Perfume and Cologne
Crazy Pet, Fresh Pet, and Unleashed Perfume and Cologne
Groomers
888.704.7666
www.groomers.com

Shampoos and Conditioners
Fur Butter Conditioner and Oatmeal and Perfect Coat White Peal Shampoo
Buttercup's Paw-tisserie
63 Fifth Avenue
Brooklyn, NY 11217
866.PAW.TISSerie
www.buttercupspaw.com

Pro-Line Self-Rinsing Shampoos and Styling Sprays
CherryBrook
800.524.0820
www.cherrybrook.com

Sunscreen
Pet Sunscreen SPF15
972.712.2812
www.funstuffordogs.com

Toothpaste and Dental Treats
Petrodex Enzymatic Toothpaste and ProDental Gel
ValleyVet
www.valleyvet.com

Greenies Treats and YipYap Breath Mints
Available at any pet store that sells dog and cat food.

EXERCISE

CAMP AND DAYCARE
Camp Bow Wow
877.700. BARK
www.campbowwow.com

Camp Dogwood
312.458.9549
www.campdogwood.com

Camp Winnaribbun
775.348.8412
www.campw.com

Dogtopia, A Daycare and Spa
888.DOGTOPIA
www.dogdaycare.com

CLASSES AND CLUBS
Agility
Agility Ability
www.agilityabilty.com

American Kennel Club
www.akc.org

Teamworks Agility Classes
919.855.0422
www.dogintrainingraleighnc.net

Big Air
Dock Dogs
www.dockdogs.com

Doga
DogaDog
www.dogadog.com

Flyball
Flyball Dogs
www.flyballdogs.com

Search-and-Rescue
Search Dog Foundation
206 N. Signal St., Suite R
Ojai, CA 93023
888.459.4376
www.searchdogfoundation.org

GYMS, MASSAGE THERAPY, AND SPAS
Biscuits and Bath
212.419.2500
www.biscuitsandbath.com

Canine Fitness Center
1353 Generals Highway
Crownsville, MD 21032
www.caninefitnesscenter.com

Courteous Canine
3414 Melissa Country Way
Lutz, FL 33559
813.949.1465
www.courteouscanine.com

Georgia Dog Gym
35 Fred Kelly Road
Rome, GA 30161
706.378.BARK
www.theatlantadogtrainer.com

Pup n Iron
www.pupniron.com

FASHION AND ACCESSORIES

PRODUCTS
Adventure Gear
Ruff Wear
888.783.3932
www.ruffwear.com

Waggle
www.wagglestore.com

Apparel, Specialty
Note: All of the apparel products below can be found at most pet stores. See General Store Directory for more information and to find a store closest to you.

Designer
Doggie Designer
www.doggiedesigner.com

Hello, Kitty!
Paw Palace
www.pawpalce.online.com

Casual
Barkus Pet Boutique
www.barkuspet.com

Casual Canine and East Side Collection
www.thepuppyshop.com/casual.htm

Costumes
Extreme Halloween
www.extremehalloween.com

Your Breed Clothing Company
www.yourbreed.com

Wiggle-n-Waggle
www.wiggle-n-waggle.com

Carriers
Road Hound Moto-Pets Accessories
866.310.2991
www.road-hound.com

Sherpa Pet
973.625.5900
www.sherpapet.com

Collars and Leashes
DogLA
www.dogla.com

Paco
www.pacocollars.com

Retro Pet
www.retro-pet.com

Rope-n-Go
888.800.5365
www.ropengo.com

Tail Wags
Ketchum, ID
866.726.WAGS
www.tailwags.com

Walk-e-Woo
67 West Archer Place
Denver, CO 80223
303-717-2386
www.walkewoo.com

Food Storage
Perfect Petfeeder
www.perfectpetfeeder.com

GPS Location Device
Global Pet Finder
www.globalpetfinder.com

ID Tags
Customized Tags
909.483.7925
www.1cutepooch.com

Fetching Tags
404.523.3331
www.fetchingtags.net

Sterling Silver Dog Tags
www.doggieid.com

Muzzles
Happy Muzzle
415.861.4724
www.doginthecity.net

FURNITURE

PRODUCTS AND STORES
Beds
Canine Cooler Bed
Pets 4 You
pets4you.com/pages/canine_cooler/
index.htm

*Crypton Super Fabric,
Stain-resistant Beds*
800. CRYPTON
www.cryptonfabric.com

DogBed Works
www.dogbedworks.com

Friends of Cashmere Co.
www.freindsofcashmere.com

FlexGel, Luxury Pet Beds
888.435.2337
www.flexgelluxurypetbeds.com

Kuddle Kots, Holistic Pet Beds
888.358.3353
www.kuddlekots.com

Orthopedic Heat and Wellness Bed
Mighty Pets
www.mightypets.com

Crates
Designer Crate Covers
www.cratecoversandmore.com

*Hardwood Hideaway, Designer Dog
Crate and Fine Furniture*
www.hardwoodhideaway.com
Catalina Collection Bedroom Set

Doors
Hale Pet Doors
800.646.4773
www.halepetdoor.com

FOOD AND VITAMIN SUPPLEMENTS

PRODUCTS AND STORES
Food, High Quality and Holistic
Avoderm
800.255.4286
www.breeders-choice.com

Blue for Dogs
www.bluebuff.com

Treats, Cakes, and Cookies, All-Natural
Bubba Rose Biscuit Company
www.bubbarosebiscuitco.com

Dogswell
888.559.8833
www.dogswell.com

Happy Tail Ale
www.beerfordogs.com

Kool Dog Kafe
www.kooldogkafe.com

Ma Snax
www.masnax.com

Robbie Dawg
www.robbiedawg.com

Stella & Chewy's
www.stellaandchewys.com

Three Dog Bakery
www.threedog.com

Trudy's
www.trudyshomemade.com

Supplements
*Note: The best online pet pharmacy is
PetMeds. This store can readily supply
any supplementary need. See Store
Directory for contact information.*

SPECIALISTS

ANIMAL COMMUNICATORS
Carol Gurney
3715 North Cornell Road
Agoura, CA 91301
818.597.1154
www.animalcommunicator.net

Lydia Hiby
760.796.4304
www.lydiahiby.com

Etiquette Coaches
*See Schools, Obedience to find an ani-
mal behaviorist/coach in your area*

Fitness Experts
*See listings for Exercise, Gyms to find an
animal fitness expert in your area*

TRAINING
SCHOOLS AND CLASSES
Assistance and Seeing Eye Dog Training School

Assistance Dog International's Directory of Membership Organizations
www.adioline.org

International Guide Dog Federation
Hillfields, Burghfield Common
Reading, UK RG7 3YG
+44 118 983 1990
www.ifgdsb.org.uk

The Seeing Eye
PO Box 375
Morristown, NJ 07963-0375
973.539.4425
www.seeingeye.com

Obedience Training
Behavior Boot Camp
Diana L. Guerrero
760.875.6874
www.arkanimals.com

Better Dog Training
www.doganswers.com

K-9 Camp
302.456.3160
www.k9camptraining.com

PetSmart
www.training.petsmart.com

PRODUCTS
Note: Training products can be found at most pet stores. See Store Directory for contact information.

Housebreaking Pads and Diapers
Pet Gold Puppy Training Pads
Simple Solution Diaper Garment
Wee-Wee Pads

Training Aid
Bitter Apple Spray
Premier Gentle Spray Bark Control

TRAVEL
PET-CHAFFEUR SERVICE
Pet Chaffeur
www.petride.com

Pet Taxi
www.pettaxi.com

PET-FRIENDLY ACCOMMODATIONS
Pet Friendly Travel
www.petfriendlytravel.com

TRAVEL CARRIER
Pet Flys
www.petflys.com

GENERAL STORE DIRECTORY
A Bone to Pick
410.451.4494
www.abone-to-pick.com

Bailey and Wags
800.887.5448
www.baileyandwags.com

Barker and Meowsky
1003 W. Armitage Avenue
Chicago, IL 60614
773.868.0200
www.barkerandmeowsky.com

Bow Meow
www.shopbowmeow.net

Charming Pet Products
www.charmingpetproducts

Holden Designs
310.391.5509
www.holdendesigns.com

Isabella Cane
www.isabellacane.com

Lead Your Human
www.leadyourhuman.com

Planet Dog
800.381.1516
www.planetdog.com

PetCo
www.petco.com

PetEdge
800.698.9062
www.petedge.com

PetMeds
www.petmeds.com

Raising Rover
Jeff Silverstein and Frank Foronjy
1428 Lexington Avenue
New York, NY 10128
212.987.7683

Red Dog
800.petmeds
www.reddogbowtie.com

Target
www.target.com

Wag-n-Wash
www.wagnwash.com